Bibliographic information published by the German National Library:

The German National Library lists this publication in the National Bibliography; detailed bibliographic data are available on the Internet at http://dnb.dnb.de .

Imprint:

Copyright © 1993 GRIN Verlag
Print and binding: Books on Demand GmbH, Norderstedt Germany
ISBN: 9783668600539

This book at GRIN:

https://www.grin.com/document/385498

Eugenia Petropoulou

Different Patterns of Female Labour Force Participation in Third World Countries

GRIN Verlag

GRIN - Your knowledge has value

Since its foundation in 1998, GRIN has specialized in publishing academic texts by students, college teachers and other academics as e-book and printed book. The website www.grin.com is an ideal platform for presenting term papers, final papers, scientific essays, dissertations and specialist books.

Visit us on the internet:

http://www.grin.com/

http://www.facebook.com/grincom

http://www.twitter.com/grin_com

DIFFERENT PATTERNS OF FEMALE LABOUR FORCE

PARTICIPATION IN THIRD WORLD COUNTRIES:

A COMPARATIVE STUDY

by

EUGENIA PETROPOULOU, B.A.

A Dissertation Presented in Partial Fulfillment of the Requirements for the Degree

Master of Arts

1993

Depatment of Sociology and Social Policy

University of Durham, Durham, United Kingdom

DEDICATION

TO

MY MOTHER, FATHER, SISTER

AND

GEORGE

ABSTRACT

Attempts to account for the prevalence of women's inferior position in the home or in the labour markets still leave unexplained the persistence of inequalities between the sexes in both domains despite the presence of increasing female labour force participation. The study assesses the importance and extend to which women's life cycle variables shape their economic activity and perpetuate their subordination.

Finally, the analysis suggests that ideological or cultural structures are the more important correlates of women's economic activity and that life-cycle variables cannot adequately account for the persistence of their low status in the labour force.

ACKNOWLEDGEMENTS

I wish to express my sincere gratitude to my supervisor Dr. Pandeli Glavanis for his comments, guidance, patience and encouragement at all stages of this research.

Special thanks are due to all my friends who in diverse ways contributed to this study. In particular, I am grateful to Alexander Iskandar who gave of his time to perfectionate the technical part of this dissertation and both to Nilaycan and Su-Chen for their emotional support.

TABLE OF CONTENTS

LIST OF TABLES

DIFFERENT PATTERNS OF FEMALE LABOUR FORCE PARTICIPATION IN THIRD WORLD COUNTRIES: A COMPARATIVE STUDY

INTRODUCTION

The main purpose of this dissertation is to study the transformations experienced by the rural female labour force in particular Third World Countries/Geographic Regions (i.e., Africa, Asia, Latin America and the Middle East).

The principle premise of this study, therefore, is to analyse changes in the degree of participation of women within the domestic sector, while market activities will be also considered, especially when the analysis is focused on those women performing dual roles.

In analysing trends in the extent of female labour force participation and the nature of the sexual division of labour, both within the labour market and within the household it is essential to test the following hypothesis: -conditioned by their need to combine their domestic and labour market roles, women who enter the labour market tend to choose occupations deemed to be compatible with domestic responsibilities; and that the sex-differentiation of roles within the home imply that women's participation compared to that of men in the labour force is influenced more by life cycle variables than any other variables.

Specifically, the hypothesis that life cycle variables such as age, marital status and maternal status, which have been assumed to influence women's labour force participation, are too weak to support our assumption.

Consequently, the objective of this study is to investigate the relationship between those factors (i.e., economic, ideological, cultural etc.) which influence the economic activity of females and contribute to their continuous subordination.

However, what should also be considered is the expansion of the world market which implicitly impinged on the life of virtually every human being, and has be accompanied by unprecedented changes in the way work is structured around the world.

The experience of women under the European empires was diverse indeed, but commonly they lost relative to men, and often this was through the imposition of a new, 'western' gender ideology (Momsen & Townsend, 1987, p.72). Colonial rule, direct or indirect, was carried out through male hierarchies; the new sources of cash, in cash crops or in wage labour or plantations, in mines or in towns were overwhelmingly imposed on or offered to men.

Moreover, the effect of the colonial period was to create a rural structure which had a great deal in common with European feudalism, where large landowners extracted surplus from a peasantry, and were the unit of production and consumption amongst the peasantry was the household. Thus, in rural areas the penetration of capitalist relations has resulted in the differentiation of the peasantry and for poor peasants, the undermining of household production and the impoverishment and the proletarianisation of large sections of the rural populations (Charles, 1993).

This has had a contradictory impact on gender divisions of labour, depending upon the position of individuals and households in the class structure. Rural households are not harmonious, egalitarian social units, but hierarchical structures embodying relations of subordination and domination based on gender and age.

The theoretical premise of chapters One and Two, therefore, despite their length, is that the subordination of women in the rural areas of the Third World has two aspects. First, women are members of households that differ in their access to land, other means of production, and wage incomes (i.e., transition from subsistence to a market economy);

and second, that the peasant household transformed its form and functions, implying both alterations in gender divisions and a decrease in patriarchal control over its members.

In Chapter Three we test the hypothesis of the study, and argue that despite the patriarchal dissolution and woman's increasing economic activity, her position within the household or in the market still remains subordinate to that of man's. This entails a theoretical discussion of woman's subordination within the sexual division of labour, extending from preclass hunting-gathering societies to capitalist or Third World societies.

In Chapter Four we illustrate the characteristics of patriarchal control which took a new form as they now incorporated with the peculiar features of colonialism and capitalism, which continue to impinge women's economic activity and therefore generate their subordination.

In the concluding chapter we examine how different ideological mechanisms accompanied by distorting customs legitimise woman's oppression.

The overt use of ideology as a means of instituting compliance is particularly revealing of the connection of between colonisation and the deterioration of personal relations. It also reveals the connection between the economic exploitation of both sexes and the subordination of women and between sexual inequality and other forms of inequality (Ettiene, 1980).

It is what many feminists have argued, that capitalism cannot exist without *patriarchal relations:* that is, the institutionalised patterns and ideologies of male dominance and control over resources that have empowered men to define the productive and reproductive roles and behaviour of women. Whether or not they are essential, patriarchal relations have become the highly characteristic of the whole modern, urban, industrial world - and of the Third World.

CHAPTER ONE

THE EFFECTS OF THE PENETRATION OF THE MARKET IN RURAL HOUSEHOLDS

A. Introduction

The next two sections will explore the changes in gender divisions of labour which are consequent upon colonial expansion and the incorporation of pre-capitalist or non-capitalist societies into a capitalist world economic order. This process has emerged along with the intellectual curiosity of the study of rural transformations and impose questions of how capitalism penetrates and transforms rural structures and what are the consequences of this transformation for both capitalism and the structures that are being transformed by it.

Existing advanced industrial societies (socialist and capitalist) emerged from agrarian societies in most of which patriarchal peasant production based on the household[1] prevailed; women's labour was controlled by men; large landowning strata or classes extracted a surplus from the peasantry; and gender ideologies defining women's role as purely reproductive predominated (Moore, 1967). In the sixteenth-century England the landowning class saw the commercial opportunities presented by the wool trade and enclosures deprived the peasantry of their livelihood forcing them off the land and into the ranks of the agricultural workforce. This term was termed primitive accumulation by Marx (Marx, 1976a).

The peasantry no longer a peasantry in the strict sense of the term, had to work for wages in order to buy the food they had previously been able to grow themselves and, in

---

[1]. Households, Family structures and the Domestic domain have an equivalent meaning in this project.

1

this way, a home market was created, a market for goods produced in capitalist agriculture and industry.

In the Third World it was the colonial expansion which paved the way for subsequent capitalist development. This is accounting not only in the agrarian societies but in those based on shifting agriculture and foraging where women enjoy a relatively high degree of autonomy in the labour process, have independent access to productive resources, and production may be neither household based nor controlled by a male head of household.

Nash has defined the process of development in the Third World as 'a process that displaces rural populations from a given subsistence mode of production (and) that fails to re-integrate people into new forms of employment' (Nash, 1986, p.6). In other words it reinforces the simultaneous destruction of pre-capitalist or non-capitalist modes of production[2] and the integration of societies into the capitalist economy. The basic change that occurs is that, instead of production being adapted to the production of use-values (production for consumption) with some production of commodities for exchange, commodity production becomes generalised. Thus, instead of people's being able to produce enough food and other subsistence articles to meet their own needs through limited exchange, they are forced to meet their subsistence needs through the cash economy. These processes according to Charles were set in train by colonial expansion (Charles, 1993).

From the point of view of the colonising power, the colonies were regarded as both a source of raw materials and a potential market for manufactured goods as the industrialised countries' markets were increasingly saturated with the necessary consumer goods (Ettienne, 1980). The labour force for the extraction of raw materials or the

---

[2]. A mode of production has generally been defined through the combination and articulation of two other concepts: 1) productive forces, that would include a technological level of the means of production and organisation of labour power, and 2) the relations of production (relations that men set up among themselves) in the process of social production. The productive forces and the relations of production take on certain possible modes in different historical periods (Abercrombie et. al., 1988).

cultivation of crops for export was to be provided by the indigenous population. To encourage their participation they were required to pay taxes which served as a means of both raising revenue and of forcing their participation in the cash economy. To pay the taxes people had to have access to cash, either through selling their labour power or through selling their products. They could not continue to produce and trade in the ways to which they were accustomed.

There are certain measures which the colonial powers adopted in order to obtain control over the indigenous population and which had significant implications for gender divisions. These measures were firstly, the imposition of taxes normally payable by adult men. It was assumed by the colonial powers that men were heads of households and women were dependent upon them; this is why men were taxed rather than women. Secondly, private property in land was introduced. This very often involved giving title to men regardless of the systems of inheritance and patterns of land use which actually obtained. These measures meant that men had to obtain cash to pay taxes either through working for a wage or growing a crop which could be solved; that is a cash crop which could be exported. Manufactured goods from the colonising power became available, undermining the handicraft production of the indigenous population (Charles, 1993). The disruption of the indigenous mode of production included in these processes gave rise to male control of female labour in societies where it had previously been latent or non-existent, and to new forms of male control over female labour in societies in which it had previously existed. In this way non-capitalist societies were absorbed into the cash economy and the process of the formal subsumption of labour under capital was set in train (Alavi, 1982, p.186). This process did not necessarily imply the destruction of non-capitalist forms of social organisation but simply that these forms were being transformed from within by capitalist production relations.

With land reform, which has occurred in many Third World countries, the penetration of agriculture by capital becomes more rapid. It is no longer impeded by forms of land ownership and tenancy that are non-capitalist in nature, and the differentiation of the peasantry and proletarianisation and pauperisation[3] of a large proportion of the rural population proceeds apace. This process has been accelerated by the introduction of modern technology into agriculture, the most well known example being the Green Revolution technology in India and other parts of Asia. This marks the real subsumption of labour under capital (Alavi, 1982, pp.186-88).

Moreover, this (rural) transformation, which is going to be more elaborated in section B, brought about stratification within the rural population and a relative surplus population has been created. Also the development of commodity production and a massive rural exodus in search for jobs in urban areas has determinant implications for the sexual division of labour as will be discussed later on.

To conclude, for a complete analysis of both colonial and capital penetration in the rural sector we need to compare the economic system in the process of decline with the emerging system in Third World agriculture, which are, according to Long: subsistence production and commodity or capitalist production (Long, 1977).

A.1 Subsistence Production

According to Beneria, subsistence production is an economic system and a way of living *per se*. Its main characteristics are that it is a self-sufficient system which shows a unity in all economic activities of the peasants and hence lacks any sort of differentiation between the productive and consumptive spheres of their lives. The subjective drive behind the act of production is not to make profit through selling the products in the market but to satisfy the subsistence needs of the family. Because of this underlying subjective drive, which manifests itself as a specific economic mentality, everyone tries to

---

[3]. The introduction of new technology and mechanisation and increasing dependence on production for the market, tend to increase the minimum size of the economically efficient farm. This in turn causes smaller farmers/peasants to lose land through dept, mortages, forfeitures, or sale, and this sharply increases the proportion of very small farmers on the brink of ruin and of landless labourers - a process of increasing pauperisation and proletarianisation (Gita Sen, 1985).

produce in accordance with his/her own needs, which in turn determine the value of production (Beneria, 1985).

From what is being said till now, the subsistence economy is the basic characteristic of a self-sufficient household (a model of a virtually non-existent entity) which reproduces itself fully from what it produces and is thus truly autarkic. But according to other authors, this autarkic model is largely a fantasy (Smith & Wallerstein, 1992). However, it should not therefore be forgotten that virtually every household produces some of what it requires to reproduce itself, that is produces some subsistence income.

The household may do this by hunting, gathering, or agriculture to obtain food for consumption. Obviously, this kind of household subsistence production is of diminishing significance, since the percentage of the world labour time (however remunerated) in such activities is on the decline. Household self-manufacture seems on the other hand as important a source of income as it ever was, even if the items thus produced are less likely to be the presumed basics (preserved foods, clothing, the house itself) and more likely to be the increasing number of 'do-it-yourself' manufactures (in whole, or more often in part) (Smith & Wallerstein, 1992, p.16). And household subsistence services on the other hand seems to be actually increasing overall, rather than decreasing in labour input. Households not only still for the most part prepare their own food, but they continue to 'maintain' their shelter and clothing. Indeed, they probably spend far more time maintaining their shelter and clothing as the number of appliances available to be tools in these processes increases. The tools do not seem to reduce the labour input in terms of time- probably the reverse- even if they usually make the labour input require less- muscle power. The mere listing of the multiple forms of income makes it very obvious that real income or real households is normally made up of all these components (Smith & Wallerstein, 1992, pp.16-17).

In pre-capitalist subsistence economies, most of work was done within the family unit. The household is the basic unit of production in a peasant economy and develops an integral division of labour based on age, as well as gender. It is the physical locus of both

5

production and reproduction since it is there that human life and vital capacity of work are continuously produced and reproduced. Subsistence production includes work related to pregnancy, childbirth, nursing and education of the children; it includes the work required in the production and transformation of food, clothing, housing and physical and psychical work of sexuality, in sort, women's work (as wives, housewives and mothers) (Sharma, 1984, pp.57-88). Moreover, Engels viewed the production of the means of subsistence and the reproduction of the human beings as two fundamental human/female activities (Engels, 1979, pp.3-55).

Capitalist production brings critical changes to the nature of the household unit. Work is divided into 'public socialised work, and work that remained in the family. The more development takes place, the more work that used to be done in the family is brought into wage labour' (Sharma, 1984, p.61), and the more that women increasingly are usurped from their public role in production. This does not mean, however, that housework has become unimportant.

It is at this point that it is crucial to mention the mistaken position within the Marxist tradition in terms of 'use values as such lies outside the sphere of political economy' (Marx, 1911, p.19). The negative neglect of non-commoditised sectors - such as subsistence production and the household economy - has been a common feature until recently. Moreover, the central argument implied here and continued as follows (in the commodity production sub-section) is that any conceptualisation of economic activity should include the production of use-values as well as exchange values, and that active labour should be defined in relation to its contribution to the production of goods and services for the satisfaction of human needs (Benaria, 1985). Whether this production is channelled through the market and whether it contributes directly to the accumulation process are questions that can be taken up at a different level of analysis, and should not bias our understanding of what constitutes economic activity. That is, the argument is far from implying that there is no difference between commodity and subsistence production,

6

as will be seen below but that the latter is also part of the realm of economics, and must be analysed and valued accordingly (Radcliffe, 1993).

A.2 Commodity Production

Writers on commoditisation[4] (i.e., Friedman, 1980, Long, 1984) have focused upon the process of deepening commodity relations within the reproductive cycle of the household. This process is illustrated by the household's increasing reliance upon transactions conducted through the market for the sale of produce and labour power, and for purchase of necessary consumption goods and renewal of means of production (Bernstein, 1979).

Commoditisation leads to the 'individualisation' of the household as direct reciprocal ties between units are replaced by market relations and households enter into increasing competition in their efforts to increase control over land, labour and other means of production (Friedmann, 1980, pp.158-84). While the commoditisation approach is a valuable tool for analysing the ways in which households as units of production are incorporated into the market and subordinated to capital, it contains serious limitations in its ability to reveal the changing roles and circumstances within the domestic unit. In particular, the model fails to give sufficient attention to the persistence of non-commoditised (i.e., reciprocal and co-operative) labour relations, the non-monetised exchange of goods and the continued importance of use-value production (Sage, 1993).

---

[4]. The distinction between peasant and simple commodity production forms of production rests on the degree of commitment to the market. Peasants characteristically reserve some of their production for home consumption or for inter-household, non-monetary exchange, while simple commodity producers are more heavily committed to the market. The end point of commoditisation, as Friedmann puts in, is 'an enterprise, whose relations to outsiders progressively take the forms of buying, selling, and competition' (Friedmann, 1980, p.163). Simple commodity producers, then, depend to a considerable extent on commodity relations for reproduction. This is not so much the cause with peasant producers who, under certain conditions, may resist full market incorporation. Organisationally, peasant and simple commodity production may, however, be similar depending on family labour and a similar division of labour within the household. Empirically, it is often difficult, especially in Third World contexts, to differentiate between these two forms (Long, 1984, pp.26-27).

Thus, as argued previously, subsistence production and commodity production should be valued as two interrelated and supplementary processes in the capitalist mode of production and with the gradual penetration of the market into economic life we view a generating shift of production from the domestic to the market sphere.

Subsistence producers measures their product in terms of use-values; they do not calculate the exchange-value in advance. The conversion of these use-values into exchange-values is outside their control and is unfavourable to them. For example, the wage labour system, as Marx and Engels noted (In Sharma, 1984, pp. 60-1) is sustained by this very socially necessary but private (that is domestic) labour of housewives, mothers, and daughters in childbearing, rearing, cleaning, washing clothes, mending maintenance of property, food preparation, daily health care etc. This constitutes a perpetual cycle of labour necessary to maintain and perpetuate the workforce. In this sense it is an integral part of the economy. The direct consumption of commodities purchased with wages takes place within the household, yet the inputs used for domestic production are not all bought on the market; some, like wood and vegetables, may be gathered by women. These inputs are then transformed into use-values (via food processing, cooking, etc.) by women for consumption in the home. Both types of consumption serve to reproduce the commodity labour power (Beneria and Gita Sen, 1981, p.292).

The same applies to peasants. Even when they cultivate cash-crops, a use-value-oriented way of treating the crops prevails, and it is exactly this attitude which makes this form of agricultural production so profitable (Bennholdt-Thomsen, 1982, p.246).

The producers therefore, within the capitalist mode of production are themselves in charge of the work of producing their own labour and that of their family. Capital does not assume any responsibility for it. Yet the economic aspect of the family is obscured and it comes to be regarded as 'unproductive' (not participating in wage labour). It is unpaid work which in turn, is the exact definition of surplus-labour (Secombe, 1973). The

8

petty commodity producer because he/she is *not* part of a pre-capitalist mode of production, they are increasingly forced to sell a part of their product in order to get money to buy basic provisions. This money is entirely spent on acquiring heating oil, medicines, roof tiles, etc., but not on daily food. Equally, peasants who are also wage workers pay for some necessary purchases with their wage but they have also to produce their own supplies for food. The domestic labour of women thus becomes 'unproductive' as well (Sharma, 1984, p.61). The husband's wage or salary is only spent in buying goods for the family's daily consumption. If the wife's work were to be paid from the wage, the level of the normal wage would be grossly insufficient. As the family increasingly becomes isolated from 'paid, productive, wage labour'[5], women for once more are cut off from men in a drastic new way and this gives new meaning to male supremacy within patriarchy. As Mackintosh emphasises household labour must also be seen in relation to existing cultural norms and values concerning the sexual division of labour, the obligations of marriage, and the expectations of family and kin, illustrated in the following sections (1979, p.83).

To conclude, the gradual penetration of the market into rural economies introduces different degrees of direct contact with commodity production and capital. Yet it does not

change the productive and reproductive nature of these activities; what changes is the degree of their integration into the market.

---

[5]. The concept of 'family wage' can be introduced in two ways: 1) the wage that fulfils expectations and improvements of the family standard of living, or 2) the minimum possible wage that is physically indispensable to reproduce the family's labour power. That is, the value of labour power is equivalent to '... the value of the means of subsistence necessary for the maintenance of the labourer' (Marx, K., 1976a, p.71). If the price of labour power falls below its minimum, labour can only be maintained in a 'crippled state' (Marx, K., 1976a, p.73).
Since the wage is affected by 'historical and moral' elements, (Marx, K., 1976a, p.71), it will vary accordingly to historical conditions within different societies at different levels of development.

CHAPTER TWO

THE PEASANT HOUSEHOLD AND ITS TRANSFORMATION

B. Introduction

The tendency to dehistorise household formation and functioning and to treat households as 'natural' units seems to be both persistent and widespread[1] (Harris, 1981). This is for instance, quite apparent in Sahlins' work which draws upon Chayanov's theory of peasant household (Chayanov, 1966; Shahlins, 1974). According to Shahlins formulation, economic systems which are not dominant by commodity exchange, such as primitive or peasant economies, are based on a domestic mode of production. The household unit tends towards self-sufficiency and relative autonomy. The primary premise of this model is that intrahousehold relations are based on a different logic and qualitatively differ from interhousehold relations. The former are characterised by pooling of resources and sharing while the latter are based on exchange. For example in many parts of sub-Saharan Africa, husband and wife do not pool resources, do not have a common housekeeping or child care fund and may enter into economic transaction which may take the form of commodity exchange (Kandiyoti, 1985).

Such arrangements are alien to most of Asia and the Middle East, where the total control of economic resources is generally vested in the person of a titular male head who may allocate resources from the common fund differentially to household members according to the positions they occupy in terms of sex and age.

---

[1]. Olivia Harris (1981, p.51) observes generally and in relation to women that: the 'term household denotes an institution whose primary feature is co-residence; it is overwhelmingly assumed that people who live within a single space, however that is socially defined, share in the tasks of day-to day servicing of human beings, including consumption, and organise the reproduction of the next generation'. Although membership of a household implies at least a minimal degree of interaction with others in the unit, it cannot be assumed that such interaction entails equality with others or even co-operation among individuals (Townsend and Momsen, 1987).

The issue of the relationship between economic systems and household is of major interest, but what will concern us here is the specific question of transformation, i.e. the shifts in the basis of the reproduction of the agrarian households. Changes in the conditions of the household's reproduction have direct implications both for the labour deployment of its members and for the sexual division of labour (Kandiyoti, 1985).

Households as income pooling units may be *created* by the operations of the capitalist world economy and bear a purely formal resemblance to similar structures pre-dating it (Smith & Wallerstein, 1992). Variations in householding practices[2] may be expected both between the various zones of the world economy (i.e., core, semi-peripheral, peripheral) and within them. The vast differentials in the levels of remuneration of labour power in core and peripheral areas are sustained by and find support in corresponding household practices (Townsend and Momsen, 1987).

The low wage areas of the periphery exhibit a lower level of proletarianisation which ensures the lower costs of reproduction since 'part-time' wage labourer households continue to derive some proportion of the income from production for self-provisioning.

However, since the possibility of continued total reliance on subsistence production is undermined- sometimes forcing through alienation of land, forced labour taxation, in other cases through more gradual processes of market integration resulting in the marginalisation of small producers- members of part-time wage labourer households move between different patterns of remuneration of labour (migration, seasonal work, etc.). The division of labour within such households necessarily reflects the way in which these units adapt and undergo changes in relation

---

[2]. The structural-functionalist approach has attempted to demonstrate that there is a functional 'fit' between certain types of family and society (Parsons, 1959). They have mainly dealt with two ideal-typical families: the patriarchal extended family and the contemporary nuclear family. The former pattern is prevalent in agrarian societies, based on patrilineage, and where elders have absolute authority over the younger members and males over females. This type of family performs such diverse functions as production, consumption, education, social security, protection, reproduction, psychological satisfaction etc. The contemporary nuclear family, on the other hand, is neolocal and formed by patterns who have chosen each other by mutual consent. It also appears to be relatively isolated from the wider kinship network. This family type is assumed to be dominant in industrial societies.

to new processes of production and exchange over which they generally have little control (Household Research Group, in *Family in Turkish Society*, 1985, pp.30-31).

Thus, the female farming system in Africa meant that exclusive male recruitment for work in plantations, in mines and public works at below subsistence wages could proceed with women's subsistence production ensuring the support of the family/household, the care of the sick and the aged (Boserup, 1970).

This may result in the break-up of the family unit for extended periods of time and to the prevalence of female headed households. For instance, women in Lesotho may spend an important portion of their lives away from their husbands who work in the gold mines in South Africa, and be solely responsible for rearing their children (Boserup, 1970). However, the fact that they cannot earn a living from the land makes them dependent on their husbands' wages who in tern have to rely on their family as a sole source of social security in sickness, retirement and old age. On the other hand, in Asia where full familial participation in agricultural tasks prevailed, colonial patterns of labour recruitment affected the entire household where both men and women had to intensify subsistence production and work in the export sector to meet new cash demands (Agarwal, 1986).

These examples drawn from forms of colonial exploitation provide good indications of how economic transformations build upon already existing forms of sexual division of labour, yet at the same time modify them. What is at issue is neither total continuity nor total change but a transformation of the bases of the reproduction of the household sometimes just short of the total jeopardy of such reproduction .

B.1   The 'Classic' Formation and Function of the Household

As in all traditional societies in which family/household is the basic economic unit, the extended family was the predominant type in Third World societies, and extended patrilocality and patrilinearity was the norm.

The family or household was an independent and unique institution which met all the physiological, social and psychological needs of individuals and which facilitated the reproduction of the family and society. In carrying out its primary functions, maintained a hierarchical structure which organised the division of labour among its members. In this hierarchical system known as 'patriarchy' (Mies, 1986), individuals assumed specific roles according to their demographic characteristics and different positions within the household. The demographic characteristics which contributed to the differentiation of individuals are sex, age, marital status, fertility and health.

Accordingly, men were superior in status to women, the old to the young, the married to those who were not, the ones who had children to those who did not etc. The kinship system formed by marriage and fertility and the degrees of relationships among its members also played a significant role in determining the position of individuals within the hierarchy (Brydon & Chant, 1989).

The elders who are at the top of the family hierarchy have the key roles in the decision- making mechanisms which control all family functions, primarily production. The other members carry out tasks and take up responsibilities according to their positions and under the control of the family head. In other words, the organisation of family's or household's economic activities as an independent unit is achieved through the unequal intra-familial relations. Those at the top control the labour of other family members.

The pre-capitalist family/household is in harmony with the demographic structure of the society and with the social and economic environment. The major task of elderly family members who are responsible for the domestic enterprise is to maintain 'equilibrium' between the family size and the labour force necessary for production (Caldwell, 1978). In this context, high mortality reinforces the patriarchal system. It helps to strengthen kinship relations and increases the importance attached to marriage and fertility (Özbey, in *Family in Turkish Society*, 1985). This is justified by the reproduction of males giving women the critical role of being agents of reproduction. Sons will ensure the continuity of the lineage while daughters will be exchanged at a very young age to ensure the reproduction of an other lineage. This exchange may or may not be accompanied by the brideprice (transformation of wealth) but in all cases

13

we can see the appropriation of by the patrilineage of women's production and reproduction (Kandiyoti, 1977). This key reproductive role which together with advancing age constitute the main ingredients of a women's status should not lead us to overlook their productive role and their value as labour.

Women's work in the peasant households thus combines domestic service and 'productive' work: it is often said that peasant woman must bear a 'double burden' working long hours in the farms and in the craft production and then equally in child-care food preparation, cooking, washing and cleaning for the regeneration of the labour force. Women's workload becomes lighter and her status increases along with her seniority, when she is involved in the more 'managerial' aspects of production such as the allocation and co-ordination of tasks among the younger women (Kandiyoti,1989).

Despite obvious built-in sources (i.e., wars, epidemics and natural disasters) of tension within this system its cyclical nature ensures its stability under subsistence or semi-subsistence conditions[3] since the willingness to provide for the elders ensures a future guarantee towards similar services in one's old age (Kandiyoti, 1989).

The transition of the family/household (its shift to production for the market), which has subsistence difficulties due to labour surplus[4] has to find new solutions under the prevailing social and economic conditions and will have a decisive impact on its organisation and on women's productive role.

B.2 The New Formation of the Household

Changes in rural households were first discussed by the school of economists who argued that structural differentiation in agriculture was the function of the forms of integration of this sector with capitalism (Turkish Social Association Society,1985,

---

[3]. The loss of equilibrium caused by wars, recruitment into the army, epidemics and natural disasters exert pressure on the family's subsistence. The family can overcome its internal problems of labour scarcity and difficulties with the help of the patriarchal system, because the family's need for labour is satisfied through co-operation provided by the kinship system (Caldwell, 1978).
[4]. Declining mortality damages the family's social and economic status. Labour surplus, as long as it does not increase production, makes subsistence difficult.

p.27-30). When labour becomes a commodity located outside the household, it does not only prevent the family from being an independent economic unit, but also affects its structure and functions (Toffler, 1980).

When a closed rural economy is dominant, the household engaged in subsistence production with primitive agricultural technology and domestic labour functions as an independent economic unit. Every family member has specified responsibilities, and the household head and his wife direct and control the activities of the other members. It appears that families engaged in small scale-production on their own land or as sharecroppers or tenants, are very similar to extended patriarchal families (Goode, 1963).

On the other hand, the contemporary small-scale producers who rely entirely on domestic labour are different from the small-scale producers that characterise the closed rural subsistence economy, since they are largely tied to the market. They are dependent on the market in the determination of their crop pattern and the sale of their products and, also, because of the inputs and tools they use in production. In other words, the family is no longer an independent economic unit. Furthermore families have to undergo certain structural changes in order to maintain their status, to prevent the division and loss of their land through inheritance or sale, or to provide security for their life in the future (Goode, 1963; Kandiyoti, 1985).

It has been assumed by Coale (1973), that the mortality decline in some Third World countries took place together with the acceleration of the growth of capitalism. The important point here is that pressures resulting from both the mortality decline and the development of capitalism have affected the patriarchal family simultaneously and in the same direction. This caused conflict and tension among family members, as well as creating problems in external relations. The decline in infant mortality and in child mortality meant that the younger generation adapt faster to changing conditions and 'request' further fragmentation through inheritance leading to father-son conflicts (Handwerker, 1977, p.51).

Clearly, the tensions built into the patrilocally extended household come to a head when there is no viable 'patrimony' when the younger generation has independent sources of income or when the nature of what is to be shared changes dramatically. Thus, extendedness becomes a brief phase of the domestic cycle and a married son will generally set up a separate nuclear unit after he estimates that he has contributed the cost of his wedding to the paternal household (Kandiyoti, in *Family in Turkish Society*, 1985).

The patriarchal extended household relationships may be expected to lose strength and to disappear as a result of migration. The fact that these migrants were engaged in wage labour in their places of destination can be viewed as part of the phenomenon 'liberation of labour from the household' in rural areas (Yorburg, 1973, p.45-47). These arguments are generally put forward for young men. The labour of migrant women who most often continue working at home cannot be said to have been liberated from the family as a result of migration, since they continue to be engaged in domestic activities.

Moreover, once married, a young couple looks forward to a certain amount of independence from their elders in terms of budget allocation and daily decision making. It is not uncommon to find relatively young women with small children heading their own household at a time when they would normally be serving their mother-in-law. Conversely, the expectation of ageing in an extended household surrounded by subservient brides becomes increasingly remote (Birdsall, 1976).

To conclude, economic power relations which are always to the advantage of the older generation in pre-capitalist societies take a more complex appearance in the process of rural transformation. Living as an extended family is not preferred when the economic power of the younger and the older generation is relatively equal. In the case of disequilibrium, to the advantage of the younger generation, the older generation has a lower status, and as a result an extended family pattern with weakened patriarchal features appears.

B.3 The New Function of the Household

The loss of the family's primary functions (i.e., production) is largely related to the developmental level of the capitalist economy.

In the process of rural transformation in the periphery, a diversification and an increase in production of agricultural crops was observed. Means of transportation and communication and the scope of their utilisation have increased. Formal education, and a rapid flow of migration abroad become to take place.

The households main task, now was 'adjustment' to new social conditions by undergoing changes in its structure and functions, in order to meet the needs of members and for its subsistence.

In general, the proportion of enterprises which only depend upon domestic labour in rural areas has been decreasing. Peasants involved in subsistence agriculture as tenants or sharecroppers are disappearing even faster.

Families which use domestic labour partly or do not use it at all do not have a composition as homogeneous as others. Among both 'rich peasants' (large land holdings) and 'poor peasants' (small family farms), for example, domestic labour is partly used in production. The importance of the family's production function may diminish depending on the extent of domestic labour used, but it should be kept in mind that similar changes observed in the family's production function may be caused by different factors in different social strata (Goode, 1963, pp.35-47).

Kandiyoti (1989) asserts that 'rich peasants' utilise domestic labour even though they hire wage labour, thus earning a small-scale producer's income in addition to making profit, while 'landlords' and 'capitalist farmers' only get a profit. Yet it is those same households that are able to withdraw their women from the production process either because of their ability to use hired help or because they cultivate crops amenable to capital intensive labour saving technology. The important point here is the utilisation of only the adult male manpower of the family when the economic level is high (Townsend and Momsen, 1987).

In studying changes in the family's production function, the criterion whether the family members partially or entirely work for others should be taken into account, in addition to the criterion of use of domestic labour in production.

'Poor families' who do not own land sufficient for their subsistence and who, consequently, do not need the labour of all family members can survive by selling their domestic labour to other enterprises. As a result they produce both for themselves and for others. Some of these families are engaged in seasonal agriculture wage labour as a family and, during off-season periods, farm their own lands. Almost all family members- men, women, children- can contribute to the family's subsistence as family labour or by selling their labour (Melhuus,1984, p.109).

For some 'poor peasants', however, there is a differentiation made between family members who participate in production as 'domestic labour'. For example, in India, while women and children are entirely responsible for rice production, men do temporary or permanent non-agricultural work in surrounding areas (Agarwal, 1986, p.73).

Another type of differentiation observed, involves older family members working in family agriculture and the young engaged in paid employment. This is important because it indicates the existence of a selectivity by sex and age in the process of 'liberation of labour from the family' (Yorburg, 1973, p.45). However, contrary to the observations in large enterprises, the status of domestic labour in these families is low. In non-mechanised family agriculture, and even in such labour-intensive of agriculture as tobacco (Melhuus, 1984) and rice production (Agarwal, 1986), the labour of male members is used in less than that of females.

The importance of the production function in families doing production partly for others and partly for the family changes according to the income derived from different sources as a proportions of their total income. As the share of earnings from small-scale production declines and as family's economic level rises, the importance of

18

the family's production function decreases. Thus, the family ceases to be a production unit and turns into subsistence unit where the incomes of members earned in different ways are pooled (Wolf, 1966).

Men shift to agricultural and non-agricultural wage labour in rural areas and also begin to settle in cities, becoming entirely separated from the village. Women, on the other hand, continue to participate in agriculture or in the activities of 'housework' (Brydon and Chant, 1989). The preparation of food stuffs (i.e., tomato, paste etc.), looking after animals, the production of items for domestic use such as quilts and carpets are examples of such activities. Even when women are excluded from agricultural production, many are involved, in, at least, one or more of these activities. Thus, even rural women, who perceive themselves as 'housewives', undertake activities which maintain the family's production function in rural areas.

In conclusion, the participation of family members in production and 'working for others' are both evidence of the changes in the family's production function and of a differentiation in the characteristics of the rural labour force in response to the particular modes of production. With the increase of wage labour and non-agricultural labour, male labour has turned towards enterprises outside the family whereas female labour has remained in agriculture and in domestic work. These developments (that both alter the forms and functions of the peasant household), at first sight seem to favour the earlier emancipation of younger male (decline in patriarchal control), it does have an effect on women through complementarity. But the patriarchal dissolution for them may be superseded by the novel forms of exploitation, as described in the following sections.

CHAPTER THREE

THE CENTRALITY OF WOMEN'S LABOUR AND THE PATRIARCHAL

DISSOLUTION - A PARADOX

C. Introduction

The traditional rural household (i.e., its functions and structure) is far from being a static unit of production and consumption; the household is subject to changes- for example, in the quantity and quality of housework and in the intensity of reproduction activities- whose roots are in the sphere of accumulation.

When capitalism penetrates into the rural areas of the Third World through the introduction of industrial products or through the development of national and international markets, the households intra/inter structures and functions are altered. As a consequence, the emergence of capitalism in these areas threatened the patriarchal control of the household based on institutional authority as it destroyed many old institutions and created new ones, such as a 'free' market labour. It threatened to bring all women and children in the labour force and hence to destroy the family and the basis of the power of men over women (i.e., the control over their labour power in the family) (Hartmann, 1979, p.103).

It should also be considered that the penetration of industrial products into rural areas may take place together with the increasing incorporation of the peasant sector into the market economy and with an increase in the monetisation of the rural economy. This means that both men and women in order to survive under the new economic system, have to enter into the capitalist relations of production either through petty commodity production and trading or through cash-crop production and wage labour. Previously for production to be possible, the lineage was required to distribute land, and women and men, through marriage and kinship relations, cooperated to produce what was necessary for survival and for social reproduction (see chapter two). Now the lineage is no longer significant. Land is privatised (through new colonial measures) and can be bought and sold as the small peasant households become increasingly indebted. This meant that men had to obtain cash to pay taxes either through working for a wage or growing a crop which could be sold or exported.

The introduction of a cash economy and men's introduction in it, either through growing cash crops or through wage-labour, often involving migration, gave men access to cash but, because of the separate responsibility of husband and wife, this did not mean that it would be shared with their wives or used to feed their children. As Mies (1985, p.67) states: 'Often the men find difficult to make enough money to send to their wives in the village'. Therefore, the women often without any means of production turn to begging, to prostitution, or to employment for less than the minimum wage. In any case they become the main bread-winners of the broken family[1]. Women from the poorest strata may thus be forced to seek gang work on construction projects and public-works schemes, and far from becoming domesticated, become literally 'defeminised', in the sense that in order to exist they must often abandon the norms around which their sexuality was constructed (Mies, 1985, pp.67-68).

These processes generated new forms of social differentiation within the rural household and weaken the community-based mutual aid mechanisms that contribute to the redistribution of the surplus among peasant households. The interrelationship between the economic, social and cultural changes may bring about a transformation in residential, kinship, inheritance and marriage patterns; alter, as already seen, the availability of resources and labour within the households, lead to reorganisation of intra-family division of labour; and necessitate the migration of members of peasant domestic groups (Boserup, 1970).

---

[1]. The sharp rise in landless labourers has nevertheless meant that the increasing number of rural peasants cannot produce their own subsistence and are forced to buy in food.

Moreover, this dynamic process is reflected in patterns of social division of labour- that is, changes in the sexual division of labour- which sexual division of labour has long been considered a key variable in the analysis of women's subordination. In this case women may be freed from some of the old patriarchal forms of the more traditional agricultural societies- yet new forms of subordination and exploitation might appear. The latter appeared when production for the world market was introduced in the periphery, older forms of sexual division of labour were not abolished but rather, were used, reinforced and reinterpreted as will be justified in the subsequent chapter.

However, the patriarchal dissolution favoured the earlier emancipation of younger men as the new economy 'demanded' the increase of the male labour outside the household economy and in particular the labour of women. This would imply an equivalent increase on female labour force in the market and as a consequence the improvement of women's status. But according to Hartmann (1979, p.207) : 'if the theoretical tendency of pure capitalism would have been to eradicate all arbitrary differences of status among labourers, to make labourers equal in the market place, why are women still in an inferior position to men in the labour market' ? The following hypothesis will be the first attempt to express this paradox.

C. 1   Evidence of Women's Role Conflict

The objective of this section is to investigate the relationship between those factors which influence the economic activity of females and therefore try to explain the inequality between the sexes.

It has been argued that the separation of work from the home environment, a distinction which is characteristic of modernisation, puts the burden of dual responsibility on women as homemakers and wage earners (Tinker, 1976). Consequently, the ability of women to be effective competitors in the wage earning market is reduced, or better to say women enter low status occupations.

To combine their two roles effectively, women choose occupations which are compatible with the traditional female role patterns of wife and mother, which certainly impinges on their choice of job even though female participation in the labour force may have increased. In this case the occupations they choose are more closely associated with part-time work, self-employment or flexible work schedules; a woman in this dilemma will chose an occupation which is more compatible with their households obligations.

Specifically, we will test the hypothesis that life cycle variables such as age, marital status and maternal status, have found to influence women's economic activity more than that of men's.

This hypothesis is tested using data from the regions of Latin America, Asia, Africa and the Middle-East and particularly from four countries, carefully selected from each of the above regions as their major representatives. These (Chile, Ghana, Indonesia and Turkey) are countries that have some aspects in common, such as their historical and economic backgrounds, and thus make their comparison quite interesting. They have all experienced periods of colonisation and in spite of decades of attempts at industrialisation, they are still classified as 'developing'.

a. *Methodology*

Much of the methodology is exploratory: descriptive statistics such as labour force participation rates computed for age, marital status and maternal status subgroups are used in the analysis of economic activity patterns. When applicable the rates for females are compared to the male rates by computing the ratio of female to male rates. For some comparisons one or the other life cycle variable is controlled. However, the number of controls that can be applied is restricted by the sample size and the rarity of the combination of some characteristics[2].

---

[2]. The data sets consist of a 5 percent sample of the 1970 census of Chile; a 5 percent sample survey conducted in 1971 as the supplementary enquiry to the 1970 census of Ghana; a 1 percent sample of Turkey's 1970 census; and a sample of the 1971 Indonesian census. Differential sampling rates, 3.8 percent for Jakarta and 0.38 percent for other regions, were used to obtain the Public Use Sample for Indonesia.

The above information as well as the tables used, are acquired by an unpublished thesis, and are re-adjusted to the requirements of this study (Bediako, Grace A., Male-female differential status and

b. *Levels and Patterns of Economic Activity*

The activity rates presented in Table C.1 show how the male patterns of differentials contrast with the female patterns: the male rates are high and show only small variation among countries while the female rates are widely divergent. The activity rates for the male population aged 15 to 64 years range from Indonesia's 80.4 to Turkey's 89.7 percent; a difference of about 9 percentage points. These data show that 'out of the labour force rate' for males 15-64 is between 10.3 to 19.6 percent. In contrast, the activity rate of females in Ghana (the highest rate among the four countries), is almost three times the rate of females in Chile, where the female inactive rate is almost as high as the activity rate of males; and in Indonesia less than half of the women aged 15-64 are in the labour force.

The activity rate of women in Ghana is almost 80 percent of the male rate; a very high rate of activity when compared to 28 percent in Chile, 45 percent in Indonesia, and 59 percent in Turkey. The rates in Ghana and Chile are to be expected, based on the respective cultural contexts of women's economic activity (i.e., for Chile the incorporation of a patriarchal pattern inherited from Spanish culture and Roman Catholicism, and for Ghana women were economically active since from pre-colonial times because spouses maintain independent budgets and wives are required to assume part of the burden of the support of the household) (Williamson, 1970; Smock, 1977).

The results for Indonesia and Turkey suggest: i- the impact of female economic activity is greater in Indonesia than in Turkey due to the success of attempts at the reforms by the Governments of Turkey; ii- the traditional reliance on women on the incomes of men in Indonesia makes it less imperative for women to be economically active; and iii- characteristics associated with lower participation of females are more dominant in Indonesia, or conversely the characteristics which facilitate women's participation are more dominant in Turkey (Smock, 1977, pp.54-55).

---

opportunity in the labour market: A study of the correlates of occupational sex-segregation in Chile, Ghana, Indonesia and Turkey. A dissertation in Demography. University of Pennsylvania, 1988).

TABLE C.1
LABOUR FORCE PARTICIPATION RATES FOR THE POPULATION AGED 15-64 FOR AGE, AND MARITAL STATUS SUBGROUPS BY SEX CHILE, GHANA, INDONESIA AND TURKEY

Variable/ Subgroup	Chile Activity Male	Chile Rates Female	Chile Ratio F/M %	Ghana Activity Male	Ghana Rates Female	Ghana Ratio F/M %	Indonesia Activity Male	Indonesia Rates Female	Indonesia Ratio F/M %	Turkey Activity Male	Turkey Rates Female	Turkey Ratio F/M %
Population 15-64	81.1	22.7	28	85.7	66.9	78	80.4	35.8	45	89.7	52.9	59
Age:												
15-19	42.3	16.4	39	49.2	42.7	87	48.4	28.3	58	70.6	53.9	76.0
20-24	83.0	32.0	39	85.5	63.5	74	75.7	31.5	42	88.6	54.3	61.0
25-29	95.2	28.6	30	95.4	67.1	70	89.5	33.7	38	95.6	52.2	55.0
30-34	96.3	25.0	26	97.8	73.0	75	91.2	37.4	41	97.4	45.0	46.0
35-39	96.4	23.6	24	98.1	75.9	77	92.8	39.9	43	97.6	52.6	54.0
40-44	95.0	23.1	24	98.2	80.2	82	91.9	42.1	46	97.2	53.8	55.0
45-49	92.8	21.1	23	97.7	79.0	81	90.6	43.7	48	97.0	52.1	54.0
50-54	86.2	18.5	21	96.7	79.4	82	87.1	41.9	48	93.2	54.3	58.0
55-59	80.5	13.4	17	94.7	75.3	80	83.3	39.3	47	87.8	45.8	52.0
60-64	71.2	10.4	15	91.0	71.0	78	76.9	32.7	43	85.0	46.9	55.0
Marital Status:												
Single	65.1	35.2	54	68.8	45.7	66	56.7	33.2	59	74.9	54.4	73.0
Married	93.1	12.7	14	98.0	69.1	71	90.5	32.2	36	95.9	53.7	56.0
Widowed	82.2	24.6	30	90.5	67.8	75	77.3	49.7	64	84.4	39.4	47.0
Separated	87.7	47.7	54	91.9	78.0	85	..	..	:	89.9	48.1	54.0
Divorced	..	..	:	94.1	87.8	93	81.6	55.9	69			54.0

Notes: .. Not applicable/not defined.

Sources: 1970 Chile Census, Public Use Sample; 1970 Ghana Census, Supplementary Inquiry (1971); 1971 Indonesia Census, Public Use Sample; 1970 Turkey Census, Public Use Sample (Data quoted from Bediako, 1988, p.55).

The subgroup rates in Table C.1 also indicate how the distribution of certain characteristics in the population tend to influence the overall rates. For example, in Indonesia and Chile currently married women have the lowest rates of participation; in Ghana, never married women have the lowest rate (where it is supposed to have the highest rates according to our hypothesis- they are not constricted by the burden of childbearing or motherhood); in Turkey, widows have the lowest rate. In Indonesia and Turkey, however, the economic activity rate of currently married women is only one percentage point below the rate of never married women. The high rate for married women (even though they face the double burden of the housework and the market) and the low rate for widowed women in Turkey may be the result of married women being expected to make economic contribution of some sort to their husbands' family (Cosar, 1978), and widowed women are protected by religious and legal precepts which stipulate that a Moslem woman always belongs to her kinship group (Youssef, 1974, p.107).

As it can be seen, the marital status variable itself does not support very much this hypothesis. There is some role conflict between women's economic activity and their marital status but basically this is due to cultural patterns as briefly stated (see also tables C.1a-C.1d). The childbearing and motherhood status associated with marriage could be expected to introduce greater conflicts, and thus contribute to the low participation rates.

But before controlling for the maternal variable, first we should look at the age specific activity rates.

The age specific activity rates in Table C.1 show that the lowest participation rate for males is at ages 15-19, when it is expected that many males are enrolled in school. The male rates increase for all four countries until the ages 25-29, after which increases, if any, are limited. The rates remain high through ages 45-49, and decline thereafter. The decline in the male rates after age 49 can be attributed to retirement (though it is probably too early), or through involuntary withdrawal, forced by high unemployment rates and tight labour conditions.

26

The age specific activity rates for females are lower than the rates for males and the age patterns are also different. The peak in Chile occurs at ages 20-24, after which the rates decline sharply at first and more gradually later through ages 45-49, and at an increase rate beyond age 50. The Turkish pattern shows relatively stable activity rates from 15-19 through 25-29, and also between ages 35-39 and 54. In both Ghana and Indonesia, the activity rates increase (more gradually in Indonesia) from ages 15-19 to 40-44, and 45-49 in Indonesia.

The late peak patterns might indicate that women's participation is less closely related to marriage and motherhood. According to Durand (1975) this pattern appears where most women in the labour force are involved in unpaid or low wage occupations such as family workers or employed in cottage industry. Therefore the participation of women according to these late peak patterns show unexpectedly, that women's economic activities might increase but their status decrease and which economic activities are not subject to marriage or motherhood but to cultural constrains and family formations.

Thus, for one more time the evidence are not strong enough to support the hypothesis that women's role conflict is due to the life cycle variable of age, since all female age groups participate in the labour force with a small variance of participation rates.

Finally, the maternal status patterns of female economic activity rate controlling for women's age, are shown in Tables C.1a-C.1d.

According to our hypothesis the more children a woman has the less she will participate in economic activities outside the household. Contrary to this the participation rates for women in Ghana and Turkey with eight or more children are higher than the rates for zero parity children. For Chile, however, the rates decline monotically to the highest parity level and for Indonesia the rates decline between the first and the third parity while increases as the number of children also increase.

TABLE C.1a
ACTIVITY RATES OF FEMALES 15-64 BY MATERNAL STATUS
FOR AGE, AND MARITAL STATUS SUBGROUPS
CHILE, 1970

Characteristics	One	Two	Three	Four	Five	Six	Seven	Eight +
				Children	Ever	Born		
Females 15-64	29.7	20.9	17.5	13.8	11.9	10.6	9.2	7.8
Age:								
15-19	13.6	5.6	5.5	..	..	..	..	..
20-24	25.1	10.5	7.1	6.9	5.3	8.3	..	..
25-29	37.3	20.2	12.4	6.9	6.1	5.1	5.5	2.8
30-34	42.4	27.0	19.8	14.4	8.9	8.6	5.7	6.2
35-39	39.6	28.6	25.4	17.6	14.8	11.1	9.8	7.9
40-44	39.7	31.1	23.1	19.4	16.4	15.5	11.9	9.1
45-49	31.5	28.1	23.5	17.6	16.7	13.6	12.7	8.4
50-54	25.1	20.6	19.9	14.9	13.8	13.0	11.7	9.2
55-59	16.1	18.5	11.1	14.1	9.7	8.8	7.8	6.2
60-64	15.3	11.1	9.8	8.0	8.6	6.4	5.4	5.5
Marital Status:								
Single	48.8	39.8	37.2	40.7	28.7	22.3	28.2	27.9
Married	18.9	15.7	14.1	10.4	8.5	7.4	6.0	5.2
Widowed	36.9	34.1	28.8	24.9	24.1	20.2	19.6	15.2
Separated	59.5	52.1	46.9	43.7	43.0	43.0	39.1	37.6

Notes: .. Few or no women in this category.

Source: 1970 Chile Census, Public Use Sample (Data quoted from Bediako, 1988, p.75).

TABLE C.1b
ACTIVITY RATES OF FEMALES 15-64 BY MATERNAL STATUS FOR AGE, AND MARITAL STATUS SUBGROUPS
GHANA, 1971

Characteristics	None	Children Ever Born							
		One	Two	Three	Four	Five	Six	Seven	Eight +
Females 15-64	47.3	63.5	66.1	68.2	71.0	71.9	75.7	78.0	82.3
Age:									
15-19	38.0	58.3	62.7	67.9	..	..	..	..	..
20-24	60.9	61.7	64.3	68.1	68.1	67.6	72.9	..	..
25-29	68.1	65.5	64.4	65.4	68.8	70.1	71.2	74.1	68.9
30-34	71.4	69.9	70.3	68.4	72.2	72.5	74.56	77.4	79.3
35-39	73.6	74.0	69.0	70.7	70.9	72.6	79.0	78.3	80.9
40-44	75.8	76.3	70.6	73.5	78.0	75.2	77.6	81.6	85.7
45-49	76.3	72.3	72.4	75.4	74.7	74.3	77.3	79.6	83.9
50-54	71.4	77.0	74.8	72.7	73.3	74.2	78.4	78.9	85.0
55-59	71.1	77.0	68.9	69.1	70.5	68.8	70.6	75.2	81.1
60-64	71.8	64.6	68.5	64.0	65.2	63.7	70.8	71.5	76.0
Marital Status:									
Single	42.2	70.5	76.8	76.5	75.8	71.1	74.8	77.3	82.2
Married	54.9	60.3	63.5	66.2	69.4	61.8	68.7	70.9	75.9
Widowed	65.0	60.5	61.9	61.9	63.0				
Separated	63.3	75.0	76.0	76.4	82.5	81.8	81.7	87.0	85.6
Divorced	82.3	81.6	86.2	88.1	90.3	89.3	89.9	90.8	91.9

Notes: .. Too few or no women in this category.

Source: 1970 Chile Census, Public Use Sample (Data quoted from Bediako, 1988, p.76).

TABLE C.1c
ACTIVITY RATES OF FEMALES 15-64 BY MATERNAL STATUS FOR AGE, AND MARITAL STATUS SUBGROUPS INDONESIA, 1971

Characteristics	None	One	Two	Three	Four	Five	Six	Seven	Eight +
					Children Ever Born				
Females 15-64	35.8	38.6	36.1	34.5	35.7	35.2	36.6	36.8	35.4
Age:									
15-19	31.5	21.8	22.3	14.2	31.9	..	..	..	..
20-24	37.3	30.4	25.8	25.1	21.5	23.8	24.9	21.0	..
25-29	38.6	37.2	33.8	30.0	30.7	29.2	30.2	25.5	30.0
30-34	40.3	46.8	39.7	39.9	36.1	36.2	33.9	29.4	29.5
35-39	48.2	46.6	44.1	42.7	40.5	39.1	39.9	35.9	31.5
40-44	47.2	47.7	44.2	46.8	40.2	44.2	39.0	38.8	36.0
45-49	43.9	49.0	42.5	45.9	46.5	42.9	41.5	45.4	37.7
50-54	47.9	45.5	43.3	42.9	39.0	41.5	43.6	37.7	36.8
55-59	41.4	42.9	38.7	39.5	38.8	38.4	40.1	41.9	32.7
60-64	38.2	34.2	31.1	32.3	25.5	28.8	32.0	32.5	33.3
Marital Status:									
Single	..	..	..	..	..	..	..	..	..
Married	33.5	31.2	30.0	31.5	31.4	32.8	33.1	32.1	31.2
Widowed	52.9	50.6	48.7	49.3	48.7	51.5	50.6	50.2	47.0
Divorced	51.8	54.2	59.6	63.1	63.2	59.4	63.8	57.6	44.1

Notes: .. Too few or no women in this category.

Source: 1971 Indonesia Census, Public Use Sample (Data quoted from Bediako, 1988, p.77).

TABLE C.1d
ACTIVITY RATES OF FEMALES 15-64 BY MATERNAL STATUS FOR AGE, AND MARITAL STATUS SUBGROUPS
TURKEY, 1970

Characteristics	None	One	Two	Three	Four	Five	Six	Seven	Eight +
					Children Ever Born				
Females 15-64	52.9	51.0	50.0	44.3	46.5	50.3	55.7	58.1	60.3
Age:									
15-19	54.6	53.8	56.6	69.9	63.3	50.0	80.0	..	..
20-24	53.0	51.9	50.1	54.6	53.9	64.4	66.2	..	..
25-29	53.1	50.4	44.8	52.1	53.4	56.6	58.8	59.6	58.1
30-34	47.1	50.8	41.8	45.5	54.3	59.4	62.0	63.2	59.4
35-39	46.4	44.4	39.1	41.1	49.3	56.3	58.4	61.0	61.4
40-44	48.6	41.1	41.1	39.3	47.3	52.7	61.5	62.6	64.7
45-49	43.0	42.5	39.3	38.6	46.2	55.3	54.8	61.2	62.9
50-54	46.5	47.8	44.0	50.7	47.2	54.1	59.1	60.4	62.9
55-59	42.3	32.9	27.0	35.3	44.8	44.8	54.2	53.1	61.9
60-64	39.9	49.0	36.0	39.1	44.6	53.2	45.1	52.3	54.7
Marital Status:									
Single	44.1	..	..	..	..	..	..	..	..
Married	52.0	50.8	45.0	47.5	51.2	57.2	60.0	62.3	63.6
Widowed	34.7	38.3	33.4	34.5	40.3	41.3	40.2	42.2	43.7
Divorced	46.4	47.2	49.0	40.5	47.9	55.6	43.8	50.0	33.3

Notes: .. Less than 50 women in this category.

Source: 1970 Turkey Census, Public Use Sample (Data quoted from Bediako, 1988, p.78).

The patterns for the marital status are also striking. Married women (contrary to the main argument) have higher participation rates in both Ghana and Turkey than most of the other marital status groups, while for the other two countries widowed and separated or divorced women have the highest participation rates at most parities, in contrast the single women- with the less burden of domestic chores- have the lowest participation rates at most parities.

Therefore, the insufficiency of the initial hypothesis and thus the rejection of the argument that life cycle variables influence women's participation in the labour force more than any other factor, will oblige as to agree with Hartmann's statement that 'a long process of interaction between patriarchy and capitalism or the interaction of patriarchy and male workers' reinforced women's subordination both in the domestic and the labour domain, as exemplified in chapter four (1979, p.206).

Before continuing with this argument we ought to introduce a theoretical framework of the sexual division of labour and patterns of female labour force with a special emphasis on women's subordination and how this subordination generated through the years finally incorporated with the mechanisms of capitalism.

C.2 Different Patterns of Female Labour Force

Almost all studies comparing the level of economic development with the characteristics of the labour force have concentrated their attention mainly on the analysis of the male employment, emphasising the correspondence between development of the economy and the sectorial distribution of the labour force. Men are observed to have very similar patterns in their rates of activity (as already seen) in both developed and developing countries.

Female labour does not follow a pattern that can be generalised in the same way. For female labour force, there is a much wider divergence between countries at similar levels of development with respect to such factors as participation rates and duration of labour force activities. Moreover, increases in rates of female labour force participation cannot be explained simply in terms of economic development, some economically backward countries have high rates of female labour force participation, while other countries show very little expansion in the female labour force despite economic growth. There is a number of prominent studies for explaining the degrees of participation of women, but we are going to introduce the most representative to this study.

a. *Perspectives on Female Labour Force Participation: Cross Country Comparisons*

The sociological interpretation of women's participation in the non-agricultural work force has been bipolarised (Youssef, 1974, pp.2-3). One view tends to categorise female employment rates as a function of the level of economic development.

The other view emphasises that the development of the female non-agricultural labour force is contingent upon variables related to social organisation, particularly upon the prevailing family/household system (Collver and Langlois, 1962, p.371). It is thus assumed that family organisation has powerful sources of resistance and is not merely acted upon by accelerated rates of economic development. In underlining the importance of the family system as a patterning force of female employment, this view considers that a woman's first responsibility is to her home and her immediate family: 'her key roles have been and remain those of the wife, mother house makers or workers' (Collver and Langlois, 1962, p.371).

In countries where patterns of behaviour for housewives are very rigid, women will be less free to contribute to economic production. Collver and Langlois suggested four patterns of women's participation, according to the level of development of the countries and their cultural backgrounds.

i- For the highly developed counties, they argued that women's participation is high, and the desire for increasing standards of living lead women, in making choices among alternative uses of their time, to prefer paid labour over leisure and or housework. They also claimed that diminished household responsibilities also induce labour market participation. On the other hand, the lack of demand for female labour and the value systems supporting the traditional role of women, act to counter the trend toward increased participation.

ii- The second type is the predominant pattern in most Latin America countries. Young girls, mainly immigrants from rural areas are incorporated into the work force through domestic service. These countries show high rates of female participation due to the high female population engaged in domestic activities. Postponement of marriage is one of the main features.

iii- The third type is mainly found in Caribbean countries. Women's participation rate is high. The family system is weak and unstable; high rates of illegitimacy induce women to work intermittently throughout their lives. Women in this group of countries are mainly employed in commerce.

iv- The final type is characteristic of Muslim countries of the Middle East and some South East Asian countries were women's participation rate is very low, and a pattern of early marriage and female seclusion are the norm. Women are not allowed to attend any public activity and there is also a voluntary decision to avoid public participation because of the social stigma that involvement in any public activity would imply.

Industrialisation, not only in the First World, but also in developing counties, brought about far reaching changes in women's participation in economic activities outside agriculture. Correlative with the economic and occupational opportunities provided by the new economy, there was an influx of women into the gainful employment as a result of complex factors related to female emancipation and to changes of the roles in the traditional division of labour within marriage. The transition from a subsistence economy to the industrialised market levels caused a change in the structure and particularly in the functions of the family. This occurred in the wake of moving the centre of production from the household to the factory or industry supplanting the home as the source of an increasing number of services and goods. Corresponding with these changes were increased opportunities for women's education, their rights to participate in political life, and their burden of childbearing (Youssef, 1974).

This comparative study focuses more on the countries of Latin America and the Middle East. It derives broader significance from the fact that the countries of these two regions are characterised, generally, by a similar level of economic development. They have in common a lack of industrialisation, an economic dependence on the industrialised world, a rapid population increase, and a considerable degree of urbanisation.

Moreover, Youssef (1974) suggested that presently developing countries are not following the pattern of the already developed western countries. The lack of participation in the Middle East countries, for instance, isn't a reflection of higher levels of development that these countries are experiencing.

Youssef disregarded the idea that different rates of female participation in both groups of countries are due to specific differences in the organisation of their respective economies that could cause variations in the structure of the demand for female employment[3]. She offered an alternative explanation for interpreting these differences, that is intimately linked with cultural definitions and acceptance of women's roles in these societies. Middle Eastern women have quite different reactions to the labour market than Latin American women. The former have shown a strong pattern of seclusion that prevents them from participating in any activity that implies presence in public and especially contact with men.

According to Youssef, in the case of Latin American countries women's reactions to the labour market are basically related with family disorganisation and the prevalence of concensual unions that result in high rates of illegitimacy.

---

[3]. According to an analysis of the distribution of the labour force in nonagricultural activities, she found that there are no basic differences in the structure of demand for workers between Latin America and the Middle East regions, and that, between countries, there is a minimal variability in the proportion of workers in male activities. The similarity in their manpower structure 'eliminates the possibility that variations in the labour market demands are at the root of the female differential employment rates' (Youssef, 1974, p.25).

In comparing countries, the pattern of allocation of female labour force varies greatly. The trends of female labour force participation are linked according to Collver and Langlois[4] with the specific conditions of economic development of each country and of the cultural delineation of women's roles in each society (Youssef, 1974).

Implicitly most authors comparing rates of female labour force participation in different countries have in mind comparisons between countries at particular stages of development in a continuum that changes only quantitatively. For this reason the validity of these comparisons is doubtful.

b. *Interpretations of the Origin of the Subordination of Women Within the Sexual Division of Labour.*

i- Overview

Nearly all studies of female labour force participation, both in developed and developing countries, have taken as given those conditions whose origins must be understood in order to account for the socio-economic status of women in relation to men, both within and outside the labour market.

The foregoing section of this chapter will summarise some leading lines of thought that have addressed the issue of the origin of the subordination of women within the sexual division of labour.

There has been agreement that in every society, male domination has been a pervasive phenomenon. Prehistoric evidence shows that the division of labour between sexes (Sacks, 1975) has been a prevalent situation. Historians, anthropologists etc., have agreed that the functions performed by men and women have varied within different societies in different periods of time. That is to say, what has been considered to be 'women's work' has experienced historical changes and has varied within different cultures.

---

[4]. They argue that economic development (high productivity per worker and intensive technology) increases women's rate of participation in every sector of the economy, except personal services, which diminishes substantially. Although development expands the number of workers in the manufacturing sector employment grows only in a moderate way. The reallocation of female labour is directed mainly towards the commercial sector. In earlier stages of development, women were engaged more in manufacturing than in commerce, while the process was reversed in the later stages of development.

Although the division of labour between sexes has been the result of a social division of labour that has prevailed within the framework of basic institutions like the family, the state etc., discriminatory practices towards women have persisted in most cultures and in many modern societies, and archaic laws still remain as a detrimental factor for the equality of sexes. Although improvements have occurred in many societies, women still occupy a subordinate position in relation to men.

ii- Engels' Interpretation of the Origin of the Family

In his *Origin of the Family, Private Property and the State*, Engels argued that the subordinate position of women historically arose together with the introduction of private property. The international transfer of individual hereditary property rights presupposed the identification of paternity, which according to Engels, required the establishment of control over sexual reproduction via the institutionalisation of the family. Engels maintained that in preclass hunting and gathering societies sexual equality was the norm although a sexual division of labour existed. With the introduction of the single monogamous family, a fundamental change was brought about:

> Household management lost its public character.
> It no longer concerned society. It became a
> *private service* (italics in the original); the wife
> become the head servant, excluded from all
> participation in social production (Engels, 1972, p.137).

iii- Critiques of Engels

Engels work has been subjected to numerous critiques and revisions. According to de Beauvoir (1974), Engels does not explain how the passage from a regime of community ownership to a regime of private property took place. There is no basis, according to de Beauvoir upon which to directly link the oppression of women with the institution of private property. De Beauvoir emphasised that pregnancy, childbirth and menstruation reduced women's capacity for work and increased their dependency on men.

> Maternity dooms women to a sedentary existence
> so it is natural that she remains at the hearth
> while man hunts, goes fishing and makes war (De Beauvoir, 1974, p.100).

Moreover, she argues that there is no historical evidence that smaller muscular and respiratory capacity of women has been the result rather than a cause of their subordinate position. De Beauvoir makes a point that is not explicit in Engel's writings, namely that the division of labour occurred as a consequence of the invention of new tools.

The main point for Sack's (1975) criticism of Engels is that in most classless societies, that lack private property, women are not completely equal. Moreover, Sacks adds that people do not produce spontaneous surplus as Engels has implied, but instead usually they have been economically constrained to produce more.

For Sacks, the lack of property in nonclass societies does not seem to be a sufficient reason to justify male supremacy. In many class societies, she argues, women that own private property have a substantial amount of domestic power. But class societies increase the acute division between the domestic and the public sphere, and domestic power is not translated into social power.

In class society, the rulers selected men for social production because, adds Sacks, they were more 'mobile' than women, but more than that, because they could be more easily exploited, since women had to nurse and rear children. Because men were more directly and collectively exploited, women became more restricted to household activities that did not produce nor own means of production. As a consequence, women were relegated to the bottom of the social ladder; their isolation and exclusion from socialised work transformed women into a more conservative force; and the family became the only agency involved in the maintenance of the family and the only institution responsible for the reproduction of the family and the labour power.

With the process of industrialisation women have become more involved in wage labour, but the burden of domestic activities has remained their exclusive responsibility.

Beneria, (1979) has emphasised that the control of women's reproductive activities is the central point around which to focus the analysis of women's subordinate position. She argued that the development of the control over reproduction need not be linked to the introduction of private property, since an intergenerational transfer of privilege generates the need to identify paternity. She adds that many differences exist in the type of work that women exercise according to their class position and that the issue of class should be considered in addition to sex subordination.

Gough (1975), states that contrary to Engel's idea of equality among sexes in early stages of development, in almost every society women have had a subordinate position in certain key areas of status, mobility and public leadership. These inequalities were based according to Gough, on long periods of child rearing combined with the demands of primitive technology.

C.3 Changes in Forms of Production in Peripheral Economies and the Participation of Women

Two functional causes of the division of labour among sexes are, changes in farming techniques, and changes in the population.

In agricultural subsistence economies the system of farming can be male and/or female oriented. Shifts in cultivation methods is a basic determinant of changes in social relations of agricultural production among sexes (Boserup, 1970). In modern times, agriculture has become less dependent on muscular strength. However, in almost every society, mainly men have learned how to operate new types of equipment, while women have continued to work with old manual tools. Thus, through present times, it has been primarily men that have contributed to the increase in the 'productive gap', since female activities in the countryside have remained more or less static and less productive. As a corollary, the relative decline in the female labour productivity is responsible for the declining status of women in agriculture.

In peripheral countries there exists two main types of systems of agricultural production: in the first type, wage labourers are few and women are very active in agricultural production; in the second type, the supply of male wage earners is abundant and women have little participation. In the second case, women work as casual workers. There are countries in which rural women are involved only marginally in farming activities.

During the period of colonisation, Europeans accustomed to the male farming system in their own countries, tended to modify original patterns of female agricultural production. According to Boserup, Europeans did not instruct female cultivators when they introduced new systems of production. However, European penetration had different effects in different countries. In some African countries, most of the burden of agricultural production fell back to women, since men were recruited alone, to work as forced or voluntary labourers in heavy construction or in mining or on plantations. Instead, in Latin American countries during the Spanish domination, the original patterns of female agricultural labour was transformed into a male oriented agricultural system (Youssef, 1974).

An increase in the population in subsistence economies might produce the need for more careful preparation of soil. When the soil needs a more careful preparation, men usually assist women in the performance of hoeing. Hence, a predominantly female farming system can change into one in which both sexes share an equal footing of responsibilities and burden of field work. Increases also in population may induce men to migrate to cities to look for wage labour. Patterns of migration from rural to urban places will depend to a great extent on the characteristics of production in the agricultural sector.

Often migration tend to configurate particular forms of spatial distribution of the population according to sex. In some instances, migration from rural to urban places are predominantly masculine, in other instances, migrant women from the countryside are predominant.

Different patterns of migrations to towns have been to a great extent, a function of recruitment policies of the cities. For instance, the type of development of some cities (e.g., 'male towns') has been a characteristic of many African countries (Boserup, 1970, p.167). Instead many Latin American towns have shown a surplus of women as a consequence of a predominantly female flux from the countryside (Collver and

Langlois, 1962). Female migratory movements seem to be to some extent, the result of the dissolution of the traditional relation within the family. The family, as a productive unit, has reached a crisis due, among other reasons, to the decomposition of the agricultural structure and extreme subdivisions of land. The mass of young female migrants that go to the cities independently reflects the transformation of a mode of production and changes in the relationship between the family and the economic system. Migrant women, however, have generally be trained for very specific tasks-housework within the rural holdings. Their insertion in the urban economy is made through the transference of their capabilities as potential housewives into the urban context.

C.4 Housework and Its Function In Capitalist Societies

The subordinate role played by women in capitalist societies has been the subject of a long debate. Attempts have been made to link domestic labour with capitalist production and to explain the function of the privatised domestic labour in the process of accumulation.

The following discussion will point out different interpretations of the prevalence of housework within the capitalist mode of production, its functions and the applicability of these generalisations to peripheral capitalist countries.

a- *Characteristics of Housework*

The role of housewives as producers of use-values is very important. The commodities bought in the market often must be transformed before being consumed by the family. Hence, housework is part of the process of reproduction of labour power and reproduction of the family. Housework is performed not only for the reproduction of labour power on a daily basis, but on a generational basis as well. Housework acts directly upon commodities purchased by the worker with his wage, transforming these commodities into necessary products for the maintenance and reproduction of the whole family's existence. Domestic labour is private production, i.e., production that is not produced for the market. It entails no division of labour and labour activities are performed in isolation (or aided by members of the family).

The organisation of household production has experienced many changes: i- many use values previously produced at home are now socialised (e.g., feeding, cleaning, education etc.); ii- standards and emphasis of certain domestic tasks have changed (e.g., types of food prepared at home, number of hours devoted to domestic activities); and iii-increasing numbers of married women are becoming wage labourers (Coulson, Magas; and Weinwright, 1975).

b- *Housework as a mode of production*

W. Secombe (1973;1975) has argued that in the process of transformation commodities that are not finally consumable goods, houseworkers would be adding additional value to the reproduction of labour power. That is to say, when labour power is sold in the market as a commodity, housework would be a component of the value of the labour power. In this way, Secombe incorporates housework in the production of commodities, and in the creation of surplus value. The discussion of housework according to Secombe, adds value to the commodity power and thus, has been linked to the idea that domestic labour is a mode of production, or is part of the capitalist mode of production. This problem is not easy to be solved and has been criticised by many authors. What would be important is to try to link capitalism with domestic labour.

On the other hand, housework, for Molyeux, 'lies outside the sphere of commodity production and is therefore not itself governed by the law of value' (Molyneux, 1979, p.16). Domestic labour should not be assimilated to the capitalist mode of production nor should it be placed in a completely functional relation with capitalism. Molyneux points out the argument that housework benefits capital does not explain why housework is performed by women and how it is linked to structures of male domination. The existence of a family wage capable to supporting the members of the family, is a result of a conscious struggle of the workers. When women are incorporated in the labour market their wages are generally viewed as complementary to their husband's wage. The allocation of the primary wage to the husband tends to justify and reinforce structures of privilege and subordination (Molyneux, 1979).

Since women seem to be located in the least rewarded and more static jobs, the combination of poorly paid jobs and domestic duties is a powerful obstacle for women's entrance into the labour market. Thus, the labour market complements and reinforces women's subordination at home.

c- *Domestic Labour in the Peripheral Capitalist Countries*

Although it is argued that household production on capitalist developed societies has similar functions in the Third World, however household activities in the latter show some significant differences.

Household activities in the peripheral capitalist countries can take two forms: 1- paid domestic labour, and 2- unpaid domestic labour. The first type of domestic activities is performed when one or more domestic servants produce use values for a household for a wage or an in-kind equivalent. The latter is a widespread form of female employment in many peripheral countries. These activities can not be linked with the process of production. Paid household activities do not have any direct linkage with the process of accumulation of capital.

The second form of domestic labour is the one performed directly mainly by working housewives themselves. In this case, domestic labour presents some significant differences with domestic activities performed in developed countries. First, there is a difference in the levels of technology that is applied. Most working class housewives in peripheral countries do not have access to these labour- electrical (time)- saving appliances. On the contrary, many activities are performed in the most rudimentary form, (e.g., carrying water, preparing fire for the stove, etc.). For this reason, household activities in peripheral countries are more time consuming and exhausting. In the current domestic labour literature it has been argued that domestic activities help to improve standards of living. Household activities in peripheral countries are more restricted and most of the 'family wage' has to be invested in mainly one item, that is food.

Another restriction when analysing the linkages between domestic labour and capitalism is that in peripheral countries many workers are not wage labourers but are self-employed. For this reason, the function that domestic labour performs for capitalist accumulation does not seem to be clear.

In most peripheral countries the earnings of the majority of working class male heads of the households do not constitute a 'family wage' implying either the labour force participation of other family members or starvation.

Malnutrition, high rates of mortality and morbidity in turn directly affect productivity. To make the argument that wages are kept down mainly because of domestic labour is doubtful.

Given that the deficiencies of the labour force is one of the major bottlenecks in most peripheral countries it is clear that the short-term rationality of keeping the wages below the minimum level necessary to socially reproduce the labour force is in contradiction with the long term interest of capitalist class, but one of the major characteristics of the capitalist-patriarchal corporation.

CHAPTER FOUR

PATRIARCHAL CONTROL AND ITS CHARACTERISTICS

D. Introduction

Available estimates of the world's working population grossly underestimate women's participation in economic activities and cannot tell us much about what types of tasks women perform in terms of the existing gender-related division of labour. Yet we have reached a period in history in which the most basic tenets and assumptions influencing roles and power relationships between men and women in society have been called into question, and these include once more the existing division of labour by sex (Beneria, 1980). One of the major achievements of studies of rural women in the Third World has been to integrate analyses of the sexual division of labour with changes in systems and relations of production, set against the background of differing patterns of regional and national incorporation into the world economy. On the other hand a less systematically explored aspect of the problem has to do with the mobilisation of cultural and ideological controls, and how these controls differentially mediate economic realities and transform them into concrete life options for women (see chapter five).

The foregoing case material offers important insights into this question since it covers at the very least detailed descriptions of kinship systems and the gender ideologies they embody. Yet the interaction between culture and economy is revealed as the weakest link in studies of women and development. Thus, before deconstructing the concept of patriarchy (in order to understand women's subordination which consequently reflects their low participation in the workforce), since life under different patriarchies spells important differences for women's potential for adaptation or resistance in the face of change, a feminist insight and the intersection of family, economy and gender are indebted to the analysis of women's subordination.

i- *Feminism and Patriarchy*

Patriarchy has been defined from within feminism as follows:

> Patriarchy is the power of the fathers: a familial-social, ideological, political
> system in which men - by force, direct pressure, or through ritual, tradition,
> law, language, customs, etiquette, education and the division of labour, determine
> what part women shall or shall not play, and in which the female is everywhere
> subsumed under the male... Under patriarchy I may live in *purdah* or drive a car...
> I may serve my husband his early morning coffee with the clay walls of a Berber
> village or march in an academic procession; whatever my status or situation, my
> derived economic class or my sexual preference, I live under the power of the fathers
> (Rich, 1984, p.57-88, cited in Eisenstein, 1984).

The terminology is different, but what is being described here, shows that patriarchy is notoriously difficult to define but it is usually taken to mean the dominance of all men over women and younger men (Barrett, 1980). Barrett argues that patriarchy predates capitalism, and exists also in socialist societies, and it is patriarchy that produces gender divisions. Within capitalist societies patriarchy exists in articulation with capitalism. The precise mechanisms of this articulation vary. Delphy proposes the existence of a domestic mode of production in which men as a class exploit women as a class. I n each household the husband extracts surplus labour from his wife. The capitalist mode of production is entirely separate (Delphy, 1984). Hartmann suggests that patriarchy exists in articulation with capitalism and that men have organised to ensure that they maintain particular power, both within the workforce and within the home (Hartmann, 1986).

Walby's is perhaps the most sophisticated analysis in this tradition. She argues for the existence of a particular mode of production based within the household which is articulated with patriarchal mode of production consists of a producing class, housewives or domestic labourers, and a non-producing class husbands. The housewife produces labour power in the form of her husband and children by looking after them and bringing them up. She does not, however, sell the labour power that she has produced. It is sold in exchange for a wage by her husband within the capitalist mode of production. He thereby receives payment for a commodity, labour power, that has been produced by his wife; a process analogous to the extraction of surplus labour from the wage labourer by the capitalist (Walby, 1986).

Walby continues her argument by postulating that the patriarchal mode of production is articulated with the capitalist mode of production through the husband entering the capitalist mode of production where he sells his labour power. And to ensure that women continue to serve their husbands and to create value in the patriarchal mode of production, men exclude women from paid work on the same basis as themselves. Thus, women's access to paid work, which would subsequently improve their status, is controlled by patriarchal by patriarchal relations not only within the household but also at work as well as the state.

Although the above theories are mainly referred to the developed capitalist world they can in a general level be applicable for women in the periphery.

ii- *Family, Economy and Gender*

Boserup (1970) has shown how subsistence tools affect gender stratification in foraging and hoe cultures and in societies whose technology is partly industrial (parts of Latin America and Africa).

According to Huber gender stratification or allocation of tasks have been detected in foraging, hoe plough herding and industrial societies. This theory focuses on three propositions (Huber, 1991, pp.39-41). The first one, micro level applies to the family. Those who produce foods tend to have more power and prestige than those who consume them. It is better to be able to give than to receive.

The second proposition responds to a macro-level question. What determines which sex does the most productive work? Men and women can do many kinds of work, yet in all societies most tasks are allocated by sex. However, one sex cannot perform two tasks central to group survival: no man can bear or nurse a child. This suggests a second principle: the tasks that best mesh with child rearing tend to be assigned to women. Subsistence work varies in its compatibility with child rearing. Some tasks mesh so badly that women almost never do them. For example, a hunt typically requires a uncertain number of days away from the camp. Children were breastfed to age four to increase their survival rate. A woman could not carry a nurshing on a hunt nor could she readily return to camp to feed it. Thus, women excluded from tasks that yielded the most power and prestige.

The third proposition states that in any society the most power and prestige goes to those who control the distribution of valued goods beyond the family. In foraging societies, hunters have more power than gatherers. They can distribute a large kill to the entire group. The gatherers, in contrast, can glean enough food only for the 'nuclear family'.

Thus, even from very early times women's tasks were considered less prestigious than that of men's. Women's productive work- were needed- was determined by the type of society, the type of cultivation performed and the needs of kinship in order to survive. And the hidden mechanism under these structures was and is patriarchy which collaborated with different modes of production through time and therefore transformed and reinforced women's subordination in all aspects of life, particularly in the production and reproduction spheres as exemplified in the following section.

D.1 Women as Rural Producers: A Regional Analysis of Selected Case-Studies

In attempting to present an overview of women in major regions of the developing world, we realise the risk of running into dangerous levels of generalisation. Within the broad areas specified (see below) there are not only several intra-regional and inter-community differences on the basis of religion, culture, political ideology and so on, but also significant variations in women's status according to their position in the class hierarchy. Although we will attempt to highlight the most prominent variations in each major area, given limitations of space, we will confine our descriptions to dominant characteristics at the regional level.

Our regions are primarily geographical: Africa, Asia, Latin America and the Middle East, with selected case-studies for each area.

Africa

There has been much talk, especially since the UN Decade for Women, on how women have been excluded from the development process and tend to be among the most disadvantaged of those from the poorer classes in the low income countries. ILO labour force estimates for twelve Sub-Saharan African countries give crude economic activity rates ranging from 2 to 47 for women and from 46 to 63 for men (ILO, 1977). This suggests that African women are less economically active than men. The ILO definition of economic activity is activity that produces commodities or services for exchange in the market; but excluding subsistence food production this makes the bulk of women's work invisible.

For a fuller understanding of women's role (not only in Africa but in all the prescribed regions, were applicable), and activity patterns it is necessary to consider her position within the household in terms of rights obligations, exchanges, the allocation of resources and responsibilities, and the division of labour.

The basic feature common to most African land tenure systems was that ownership was by group (lineage or community). A most important point is that land *could not be bought or sold* (Momsen & Townsend, 1987, p.149). In all African cases, inheritance was basically patrilineal. The typical pattern was that male lineage elders controlled the allocation of land among members of the patrilineal descent group.

Among the Luo and Kikuyu (east and southern Africa), women did not receive any allocation of land from their fathers' lineage, but had rights to use the family land until they married. Sons did not receive their allocations of lineage land until they married, on which their wives had clearly defined rights to farm and to control the produce (Momsen & Townsend, 1987, p.157).

A Ewe woman, in the Volta region, south-east Ghana could receive an allocation of land for her own use from either her father's or her husband's lineage; in the case of household fields from the husband's lineage, husband and wife worked together. A Kusasi woman (in north-east Ghana), before marriage, worked on the household farm, the produce of which was controlled by the male household head. After marriage she would work on her husband's household farm and she would also receive a small allocation for her husband's lineage for private use (Charles, 1993, p.104).

Among the Mandika (Gambia) there were two main forms of land use. Compound land (dryland and rice-land) was under the control of the elders and its produce was for household use. Both men and women had, with the permission of the elders, the right to clear land for individual use. This land could be exchanged or given away (but not sold) and could be inherited. Men tended to pass their private dryland fields to sons and women their private rice-fields to daughters, though this was not always possible if a daughter married into another village (Barrett and Browne, 1993, pp.87-98).

But during the colonial era, the colonial reserve system restricted the land available for allocation among lineage members. This led to an increased fragmentation of land holdings and to a weakening of lineage elder's authority, as individual household heads assumed autonomy and passed their fallow land to their own sons. The most serious undermining of women's rights to land came with the reform of land tenure. This created individual ownership of land, with the right to sell it. Land was usually restricted in the man's name, and the legal status of women's usufruct rights became uncertain. In practice women continued to cultivate land as lineage wives; but their security was removed, as absent husbands or sons could sell the land from under their feet. Women lost the important role of guardian's of their sons' land until marriage (Charles, 1993).

Pressure on land in West Africa occurred for other reasons. In the main cocoa belt, the value of land increased dramatically and a private land market developed. Migrant cocoa farmers bought up large tracts of land. Among the Ewe there was no significant private land market, but men increasingly took the most fertile forest land for their cocoa farms, thus reducing the land available for women to grow food crops. Male farmers laid claim to land in which they had invest labour, and passed on their fallow land to their sons, or that land could be sold in case when a permanent tree crop like cocoa had been planted. The introduction of claims to ownership of land undermined women's traditional rights of use. Women had previously had the right to cultivate lineage common property; now they had to get permission from individual men to use their fallow land. Also, as many women's husband were absent and thus not available to assist in cleaning land, the women's choice was further restricted to land which was easy to clear- which tended to be the least fertile (Momsen & Townsend, 1987, pp.117-20).

For example the Kusasi and Ewe population from Ghana experienced both net male out-migration and a shift of male labour at home from the traditional staple towards cash crops. In both cases, traditionally, men had the greater responsibility for the main staple; among the Kusasi for cultural reasons, and among the Ewe because of the labour needed for the yam cultivation (Momsen & Townsend, 1987, p.119). Even when women became more responsible for ensuring the household's food supply, they could not take over growing the main staple. Kusasi women had to intensify their efforts to grow groundnuts to make up shortfalls of millet during the hungry seasons; they also relied increasingly on income from petty trading to buy other foods. Ewe women relied on petty trading to supplement the household's day-to-day income (1987, pp.119-20).

It is obvious therefore, that women's work load was increased; but the extra work depended on the 'traditional' division of labour by gender and the local agricultural system. While, broadly speaking, women were responsible for the household's subsistence needs, the equation of 'male' with 'cash' and female with 'subsistence' is an oversimplification. Women in polygamous marriages after having provided food for the husband and children, they had the right to dispose of any surplus in the form of i.e., small livestock which could be exchanged for grain in bad years, thus providing some security. But her labour often crucial for men's cash crops, was unremunerated, and their cash income tended to be smaller than men's. On the other hand, male labour was withdrawn into waged employment, yet it was often more important for the household's standard of living.

TABLE D.1a
DISTRIBUTION OF THE ACTIVE FEMALE POPULATION BY ECONOMIC SECTOR[1] IN AFRICAN COUNTRIES, 1970

Country	Percentage distribution of the active female population[2] by economic sector			Percentage share of women in the total labour force of each economic sector		
	Agriculture	Industry	Services	Agriculture	Industry	Services
Angola	42.5	4.2	53.3	5.7	2.7	20.6
Benin	15.6	12.9	71.5	14.0	48.7	83.6
Botswana	93.1	0.6	6.3	56.6	9.1	35.7
Burundi	94.1	0.8	5.1	48.3	9.1	25.3
Cameroon (United Rep.)	96.4	0.6	3.0	48.2	4.0	13.7
Central African Republic	96.7	1.1	2.2	52.9	22.7	17.9
Chad	97.1	0.4	2.5	24.9	1.8	9.4
Congo	41.4	16.0	42.6	36.3	27.2	42.7
Ethiopia	85.7	6.2	8.1	35.6	37.2	28.2
Gabon	91.5	1.3	7.2	43.6	4.8	26.9
Gambia	91.2	3.8	5.0	48.7	20.0	20.8
Ghana	54.7	15.1	30.2	39.1	37.9	50.4
Guinea	92.7	5.4	1.9	44.1	25.9	10.9
Ivory Coast	86.1	0.3	13.6	44.7	5.1	46.0
Kenya	90.8	2.1	7.1	37.2	9.9	22.1
Lesotho	92.8	1.3	5.9	46.3	15.8	36.6
Liberia	89.7	1.9	8.4	38.6	5.6	22.1
Libyan Arab Jamahiriya	12.6	40.9	46.5	1.8	8.8	4.6
Madagascar	93.4	1.2	5.4	47.8	16.9	34.5
Malawi	94.2	1.1	4.7	39.9	10.7	25.0
Mali	92.1	6.2	1.7	48.0	71.8	15.7
Mauritania	95.0	1.0	3.9	4.7	-	-
Mauritius	37.8	10.3	51.9	21.8	7.8	25.0
Mozambique	94.0	1.6	4.4	32.8	32.6	8.1
Namibia	57.1	2.0	40.9	24.0	1.8	40.3
Niger	95.8	0.3	3.9	10.3	-	7.8
Nigeria	58.9	10.6	30.5	38.5	31.1	51.4
Rwanda	96.6	0.2	3.2	50.1	6.2	29.8
Senegal	89.0	2.7	8.3	43.7	15.8	23.4
Sierra Leone	82.2	4.3	13.5	40.1	10.3	34.7
Somalia	92.2	1.2	6.5	32.4	6.3	20.4
South Africa	30.9	10.6	58.5	32.9	11.8	48.6
Sudan	79.2	9.6	11.2	9.9	12.6	11.2
Swaziland	87.0	2.5	10.5	49.1	16.7	40.0
Tanzania (United Rep.)	92.3	1.6	6.1	39.3	11.5	24.7
Togo	65.0	8.8	26.2	37.3	34.4	69.9
Uganda	91.1	1.4	7.5	35.8	10.2	26.7
Upper Volta	85.2	13.1	1.7	45.8	72.4	16.9
Zaire	96.3	1.6	2.1	51.9	6.3	9.2
Zambia	69.6	5.2	25.2	31.4	19.9	45.3
Zimbabwe	68.7	6.3	25.0	32.1	13.9	32.7

Notes: 1. The composition of the economic sectors is as follows: *agriculture:* agriculture, hunting, forestry and fishing; *industry:* mining and quarrying, manufacturing, construction, electricity, gas and water; *services:* trade, transport, storage, communications and public and private services (Kandiyoti, 1985, pp.32-33).

2. Generally excluding women whose situation is not defined and women seeking work for the first time; unemployed women are also sometimes excluded (Kandiyoti, 1985, pp.32-33).

Source: ILO, *Labour Force Estimates and Projections, 1950-2000,* 2nd ed., Vol.II: *Africa,* Geneva, 1977.

Asia

In Asia, as in Africa, the bulk of women's labour force participation is concentrated in agriculture (ILO, 1977) (See Tables D.1a and D.1b respectively). Women's value in agricultural production is determined by technology (Boserup, 1970), which subsequently defines the different forms of control of female participation in agricultural production and the social status of women (i.e., classic patriarchy).

According to Boserup the operation of plough requires more physical strength than can be exerted by women; this leads to a lowering of the demand of female labour in other operations such as weeding; and ploughing is incompatible with childcare and domestic work. So female status will be lower in plough systems of cultivation than in hoe systems. South Asian agriculture is predominantly a plough system and kinship is predominantly patrilineal, barring women from inheritance; residence is patrilocal making women the virtual property of their affines, and there is a marked preference for sons, together with restrictive practices such as seclusion, making for a highly visible form of female subordination (Kandiyoti, 1985). This pattern of kinship is also predominant in East Asia. On the other hand, in South-East Asia the kinship pattern is bilateral, with rights of inheritance to women, relative flexibility of marital residence and continuing bonds between women and their own kin, particularly between mothers and daughters.

As Whyte and Whyte (1978) state, the variations in the status of women in Asia are predominantly ecologically determined. In South-East Asia, where the tropical forest cover was cleared a century ago to make way for cultivation, swidden agriculture and other more primitive forms of subsistence persisted longer. This swidden way of life gave greater independence for women whereas in several other parts of South-East Asia Muslim women owned land.

As already implied, different forms of appropriation of land and surplus have distinct implications for household formation and the appropriation of women's reproductive capacity.

TABLE D.1b
DISTRIBUTION OF THE ACTIVE FEMALE POPULATION BY ECONOMIC SECTOR[1] IN ASIAN COUNTRIES, 1970

Country	Percentage distribution of the active female population[2] by economic sector			Percentage share of women in the total labour force of each economic sector		
	Agriculture	Industry	Services	Agriculture	Industry	Services
Afghanistan	88.4	5.8	5.8	19.4	14.0	9.4
Bangladesh	90.9	3.7	5.4	17.5	17.9	8.3
Bhutan	97.3	1.1	1.6	40.1	20.0	15.8
Burma	47.6	20.5	31.9	29.5	49.2	47.0
China	78.2	15.4	6.4	43.3	28.7	20.5
Democratic Kampuchea	84.5	2.6	12.9	44.0	25.0	29.7
Hong Kong	4.6	61.2	34.2	35.7	37.7	28.2
India	80.7	10.8	8.5	37.9	26.1	16.2
Indonesia	64.9	11.3	23.8	30.4	36.0	30.8
Japan	26.5	26.1	47.4	52.8	29.7	40.4
Korea (D.P's. R)	65.2	21.2	13.6	54.7	35.2	35.4
Korea (Republic)	60.0	15.2	24.8	38.4	24.8	28.0
Lao People's Dem. Rep.	83.2	3.9	12.9	47.5	33.3	36.6
Malaysia	68.1	9.4	22.5	38.5	21.6	23.0
Mongolia	67.8	14.7	17.51	37.2	28.9	28.2
Nepal	96.8	1.3	1.9	41.6	25.4	19.0
Pakistan	69.3	16.0	15.7	10.9	7.4	6.5
Philippines	35.2	16.8	48.0	21.9	35.1	51.2
Singapore	3.1	33.7	63.2	24.0	29.1	24.9
Sri Lanka	65.6	12.9	21.5	28.2	21.4	16.8
Thailand	83.8	4.4	11.8	49.6	35.0	39.4
Viet Nam (Socialist Rep)	78.2	5.6	16.2	43.2	35.5	40.2
ASIA	73.1	14.1	12.8	38.9	27.8	24.9
WORLD	54.3	17.9	27.8	37.4	27.3	37.4

Notes: 1. The composition of the economic sectors is as follows: *agriculture:* agriculture, hunting, forestry and fishing; *industry:* mining and quarrying, manufacturing, construction, electricity, gas and water; *services:* trade, transport, storage, communications and public and private services (Kandiyoti, 1985, p.46).
2. Generally excluding women whose situation is not defined and women seeking work for the first time; unemployed women are also sometimes excluded (Kandiyoti, 1985, p.46).

Source: ILO, *Labour Force Estimates and Projections,* 1950-2000, 2nd ed., Vol.I: *Asia,* Geneva, 1977.

The patrilocally extended household is a type of domestic arrangement that is overwhelmingly associated with the reproduction of landed peasant households in economic and technical terms, but the husband father role is also reinforced by supports generated outside the household (Wolf, 1966).

For example, in China and Northern India the extended family received strong ceremonial emphasis and was found largely among middle peasants and landlords. Whether this domestic arrangement was numerically predominant or not, it certainly represented a cultural ideal. Even in post-revolutionary China where patriarchy is under attack, many studies attest to the resilience of pre-Revolutionary patriarchal features of the family and to the vitality of rural patriarchal authority (Croll, 1981a). Thus, women's subordination in Asian societies is strongly related to their position in the patrilocally extended household.

Within this system men dominated women, the old dominated the young and the needs of individual family members were subordinated to the interests of the group. Marriages were arranged by families, were ideally contracted at an early age and brides moved to their husband's village. Young women had little autonomy in either their work or their personal lives; all decisions were made by the head of household or, if they were married, their mother in law (Stacey, 1983, pp.30-34).

Ideally women in China and India were not expected to work or even to be seen outside the home and deference to male authority characterised a woman's life. Obedience was due, first to girl's father and brothers. When she married she had to obey her husband and when widowed it was the eldest sons whose authority she had to accept (Charles, 1993, pp.120-21). As in many peasant societies a woman's status improved with age and she held most authority when her son married and she became his wife's mother-in-law (Kandiyoti, 1989, cited in Glavanis & Glavanis, 1989). The extended peasant family headed by the patriarch with his sons and their wives and children residing under the same roof was the basic economic unit of society where production and consumption took place. This, of course, meant that although peasant women were subject to male authority, there were significant areas of China, for example where rice-production was predominant and women's participation in agricultural production was crucial (Charles, 1993).

In the immediate post-liberation in China reforms in Marriage Law and Land Reform were expected to alleviate women's subordination in the peasant household (Charles, 1993, pp.146-47). Free-choice of marriage and divorce were an immediate challenge to the family and to the organisation of production in China, and opposition to these challenges according to Stacey (1983) was violent resulting in the death of hundreds of thousands of women. This reaction cannot simply be understood as men opposing women's liberation but as women becoming the focus of opposition to a fundamental transformation in the family as a unit of production.

The peasant household, since the dissolution of the communes in China, has been reinforced as the basic unit of production in the countryside. Although the socialisation of domestic labour and the large-scale entry of women into production had been seen as a threat to patriarchal authority and as an advance in the emancipation of women (i.e., Great Leap Forward), women were generally to be found in the least skilled and lowest paid sectors of both urban and rural work force (Croll, 1981a).

Women's labour was crucial in the collective income-earning sector, the private sector and the domestic sector, but most significant in the income-earning sector. Thus, women and men worked on commune land, projects and industry but it was women who were responsible for the activities of the private sector, growing food and raising animals for domestic consumption and domestic labour, which included grinding corn, preserving vegetables, cooking, sewing and child care. Women working in the collective sector earned wages which made their labour visible but in the private and domestic sectors their labour was unpaid and therefore invisible. Thus women's labour was of crucial significance to the welfare of the peasant household and access to female labour was necessary for a peasant household to be viable.

Moreover, in China, the private hiring of labour had been prohibited in order to prevent the development of exploitative class relations. But at the same time the wealth and the welfare of peasant households depended upon access to the control over labour. This meant that the recruitment of labour had to take place by means other than hiring, such as marriage and the birth of children. Given the long tradition of patrilocal marriage, one way of recruiting labour into the household is to give birth to sons who can be married young and whose wives provide labour themselves and also ensure a future supply of labour by having children. In such a system daughters are considered inferior to sons because they eventually move away from their natal home while sons contribute in a permanent basis to the maintenance of the household. Croll argues that with the prohibition of hiring of labour the acquisition of daughters-in-law through marriage became the most important way of increasing the household's labour resources. So women continued to be exchanged between households and their subordination was an integral part of the peasant household (1981a, p.298).

The large extent of the Chinese case is deliberately undertaken for two reasons. First to withdraw the notion that socialism as an ideology- that emerged as a critique to capitalist society- will put an end to women's subordination and secondly, to support the premise that patriarchal control despite modernisation processes can still exist in a more 'sophisticated' form despite policies to emancipate women's burdens as we shall see in the final chapter.

Latin America

Latin America is characterised by Boserup as a region of 'male farming' although more recent research suggests that it would be more accurate to refer to it as a region of family farming (Deere & León, 1987, p.3).

During the sixteenth and seventeenth centuries, indigenous modes of production were disrupted and various relations of production (ranging from slave to semi-feudal semi-capitalist) were forcibly imposed by the indigenous population. The effect of the colonial period was to create a rural social structure which had a great deal in common with European peasantry and where the unit of production and consumption amongst the peasantry was the household. Indigenous forms of production persisted for considerable lengths of time in more inaccessible areas (Charles, 1993, pp.191-200).

In rural areas the penetration of capitalist relations has resulted in the differentiation of the peasantry and for poor peasants, the undermining of household production and the impoverishment and proletarianisation of large sections of the rural population. This had a contradictory impact on gender divisions of labour, depending upon the position of individuals and households in the class structure. In order to explore this we ought to discuss according to Charles (1993),various studies which show, firstly, that gender divisions of labour vary with class and secondly, that the continual undermining of subsistence production is leading not only to male migration as in Sub-Sahara Africa, but also to the migration of women (Young, 1982; Deere & León de Leal, 1982). Also the extent to which capitalist development in agriculture reinforces or undermines male control over female control, will be discussed.

According to ILO Estimates women do very little agricultural field work in Latin America (see Table D.1c). However, Deere has shown that the amount of work contributed by women to agricultural production, particularly in the non-wage sector, is consistently and considerably underenumerated in Latin American censuses. For instance, Peruvian census data show that the proportion of women economically active in agricultural production has declined from 19 % in 1940 to 7.3% in 1961 to 3.8% in 1972 (Deere, 1987, p.200). Deere points out that the questions asked in each census differed- in the 1940 census people were asked to describe the various 'income-generating activities' in which they were engaged whereas in the latter two they were asked their 'principal occupation'. Consequently most rural women are listed as housewives and their first responsibility is towards home and children (Deere, 1987, p.200). Cultural norms (i.e., Catholicism) require women to project what is 'right and proper'. Moreover the 1961 census required that to be considered economically active a person had to have engaged in their occupation for at least one third of a 'normal working day' during the week before the census and in the 1972 census this qualification became fifteen hours (Deere, 1987, p.201). These time limits were

TABLE D.1c
DISTRIBUTION OF THE ACTIVE FEMALE POPULATION BY ECONOMIC SECTOR[1] IN LATIN AMERICA, 1970

Country	Percentage distribution of the active female population by economic sector			Percentage share of women in the total labour force of each economic sector		
	Agriculture	Industry	Services	Agriculture	Industry	Services
Barbados	19.6	15.7	64.6	38.9	20.7	52.3
Cuba	8.1	22.1	69.8	4.9	15.2	29.7
Dominican Republic	9.4	14.1	76.5	1.7	11.0	34.7
Guadeloupe	19.2	6.7	74.1	25.0	10.0	58.0
Haiti	63.0	7.6	29.4	40.1	50.3	74.5
Jamaica	8.3	18.2	73.5	11.2	27.6	63.6
Martinique	18.7	5.6	75.7	30.8	8.3	52.4
Puerto Rico	0.7	31.6	67.7	1.5	24.2	32.1
Trinidad and Tobago	16.7	18.7	64.6	27.6	16.4	41.4
Windward Islands[2]	34.0	21.4	44.6	33.3	29.0	55.9
Other Caribbean countr.[3]	10.5	7.4	82.1	27.6	7.9	53.9
Costa Rica	4.5	17.3	78.2	1.8	15.6	37.5
El Salvador	8.9	24.6	66.5	2.8	22.6	50.0
Guatemala	8.9	22.8	68.3	1.9	16.8	40.6
Honduras	4.5	18.0	77.5	1.0	18.4	47.6
Mexico	11.1	22.0	66.9	4.2	16.8	36.4
Nicaragua	8.3	16.3	75.4	3.3	22.0	45.7
Panama	8.1	12.2	79.8	4.8	20.0	21.4
Argentina	4.2	21.0	74.8	6.4	16.1	35.9
Chile	3.2	20.4	76.4	2.9	16.1	34.9
Uruguay	2.2	23.0	74.8	0.4	20.2	38.5
Bolivia	22.2	20.9	56.9	7.8	19.5	47.6
Brazil	21.1	10.6	68.3	9.4	11.8	38.5
Colombia	6.4	22.7	70.9	4.1	26.5	42.3
Ecuador	16.5	29.1	54.4	6.2	24.9	38.8
Guyana	17.1	13.9	68.9	14.0	10.4	42.5
Paraguay	15.5	29.4	55.1	6.3	32.8	41.9
Peru	21.7	18.8	59.5	10.0	19.3	35.2
Suriname	19.3	7.7	73.0	19.0	9.1	32.6
Venezuela	3.7	16.6	79.7	3.0	14.1	34.0
LATIN AMERICA	15.7	17.1	67.2	8.2	16.7	38.4
WORLD	54.3	17.9	22.8	37.4	27.3	37.4

Notes: 1. The agricultural sector covers agriculture, forestry, hunting and fishing; the industrial sector, extractive industries, manufacturing industries, construction, electricity, gas and water; services sector, trade, transport, storage and communications, public and private services (Kandiyoti, 1985, p.61).
2. Dominican, Grenada, Saint Lucia, and Saint Vincent and the Grenadines (Kandiyti, 1985, p.61).
3. Antigua and Barbuda, Bahamas, Virgin Islands, Netherlands Antilles, Saint Christopher and Nevis, and Turks and Caicos Islands (Kandiyoti, 1985, p.61).

Source: ILO, 1977.

applied to the category unpaid farm worker, a category which includes a very large number of women. Women's agricultural work is often seasonal and they, or they husbands, are often likely to describe their main occupation as housewife, they will therefore be classified as economically inactive when in fact they are not (Deere & León de Leal, 1982).

This underenumeration of women's economic activity rates from official statistics often produce unreliable data with a consistent underestimation of women's productive activity.

Additionally in terms of gender division of labour Deere (1987) argues that this is clearly demarcated in the middle peasant and rich peasant households where it 'is not considered proper for women to participate in a good number of agricultural tasks', particularly those defined as male, whereas women from poor peasant households both make a greater contribution to family labour and perform a greater variety of agricultural tasks than do other rural women (Deere, 1987, p.206).

In another study Deere and León de Leal compared gender divisions of labour in three areas characterised by different levels of capitalist penetration. In all areas proletarianisation is taking place but its extent varies. Thus, in El Espinal (Colombia) it is most widespread, with 90% of peasant households containing one or more labour market participants while in Garcia Rovina (Colombia) only 20% of peasant households are in this situation (Deere & León de Leal, 1982, p.66). They characterise Garcia Rovira as 'non-capitalist' despite its participation in the cash economy through the production of tobacco as the main crop. This is because the majority of peasant households are independent producers and sharecropping is common. El Espinal is characterised by large capitalist farms and a peasantry concentrated on the least productive land therefore forced to sell their labour power. The third area, Cajamarca (Peru) is characterised by a modern dairy sector and a smallholding sector (Charles, 1993, p.198).

They find that in the least capitalist region women's participation in field work and marketing is low but in the other agricultural activities, processing crops, agricultural servicing and caring for animals, their participation is high. Their data also show that women's participation in agricultural field work increases with capitalist penetration of agriculture but they are significant as family labourers rather than as hired labour. This is related to the differentiation of the peasantry and women are more likely to participate in field work if they are in poor peasant households as already seen. Also the type of employment differs, with men working in the local industries and as permanent agricultural labourers while women, although they are employed in textile industry, are more likely to be found working as domestic servants, cooks, laundry workers, etc. and their pay is lower than that of men (Deere & León de Leal, 1982).

In the better-off peasant households capitalist development does not affect the gender division of labour, women remain subordinate to their husbands, carrying out their agricultural work within the domestic sphere. It is only in the households which experience proletarinisation that the gender division of labour changes, giving women a wider range of agricultural tasks to perform and transforming some of them into wage labourers as well. Their husbands move into wage-labour and therefore perform less agricultural work. In addition women's position in wage work is subordinate to that of men in terms of wages and in terms of the type of jobs in which they are employed.

Kate Young focuses on a similar process of proletarianisation or on the creation of a relative surplus population in the Mexican highlands near Oaxaca (Young, 1978).

Penetration of capitalism into the regional economy was accelerated after the 1930s by the introduction of taxes which led villagers in the more isolated regions to begin producing coffee as a cash crop. Those whose land was not suitable for coffee had to sell their labour power. Those changes resulted in stratification, with the development of a commercial class which hired labourers. 'Stressed' by the commercial class and the hired labourers, were those households (a majority) who produced for subsistence and for exchange but neither hired labour nor worked regularly for wages. A slump in coffee prices in the mid 1950s coupled with the continued need for cash and the lack of opportunities for earning it led to out migration, both seasonal and permanent (Charles, 1993, pp.194-96).

The out migration of young women occurred because they had been made redundant by the penetration of their society by capitalist economic relations. Prior to the introduction of coffee into the region, maize had been the staple crop, and cotton had been produced by the peasant women (Young, 1982). This production was undermined by the introduction of manufactured cloth and cash cropping of coffee. This reduced women's productive work in the household and their engagement in 'male' agricultural labour leading them to out migration. Young suggests that this happened because agricultural labour and village administration were 'defining features of maleness' and define a man's authority as head of the household; and secondly, because women did not have the necessary skills to participate in agricultural labour (1982. p.168). Thus, men continued to carry the burden of subsistence production while women's productive activities were undermined by the availability of manufactured goods. There was thus pressure on young men to remain in the village to carry on agricultural production where women had been made redundant and there were plenty of opportunities for their employment in towns as domestic servants.

Young argues that this process occurred as a result of capitalist penetration of a rural, subsistence economy which broke the reproductive cycle and created a relative surplus population (Young, 1982, p.171).

Young women with children or men can be separated from the household economy and therefore migrate to towns in search of employment. Kinship ties remain important and sending household members to earn money away from home, some of which they will contribute to the household, is often conceptualised as part of a household's survival strategy (Young, 1978).

What these studies show is that although capitalist development in agriculture undermines per-existing gender divisions of labour it does not necessarily undermine them in the same way. In one case women participate in 'men's' agricultural work but in the other they do not; gender ideology and the separation of male female work is not questioned because young women are sent into urban areas to do work which is regarded as 'feminine'. However, a move out of the patriarchal peasant household might provide an opportunity for the undermining of the patriarchal familial authority, although if young women go into domestic services they are simply substituting the authority of one male household head for another. Thus, although capitalist development may change the form taken by the gender division of labour, Young's study illustrate that women's subordination is maintained as capitalism incorporated with pre-existing forms of patriarchal control.

Middle East

The majority of women in the Middle East have a marginal role in agriculture according both to the stereotype and to national statistics (see Table D.1d). In the literature, the definition of the region itself may vary: it often includes North Africa (Algeria, Morocco, Tunisia) and may extent beyond the Arab Middle East and the Islamic Republic of Iran to include Pakistan. In this case we are talking about the Muslim World (Kandiyoti, 1985).

Youssef (1977) notes that not only is the overall proportion of women in agriculture low in the Muslim world, but the female workforce tends to be quite concentrated in the under-15 age group. Yet she suggests, in keeping with Boserup's typology, that the particular farming system characteristic of the region, namely plough cultivation, may be restricting women's contribution, although they are involved in light ploughing, weeding and seasonal harvest work.

This region is characterised by two rural ecotypes, the nomadic pastorals and the peasant village (Kandiyoti, 1985). Nomadic and semi-nomadic tribes are found in ecologically marginal areas of the region and on its periphery and distinguish themselves by their concentration on herding and animal raising (i.e., sheep, goats, camels), and their need to migrate between pastures to find enough grazing land for their stock. Women milk and care for animals, process milk products like butter and

TABLE D.1d
DISTRIBUTION OF THE ACTIVE FEMALE POPULATION BY ECONOMIC
SECTOR IN THE MIDDLE EAST, 1970

Country	Percentage distribution of the active female population by economic sector			Percentage share of women in the total labour force of each economic sector		
	Agriculture	Industry	Services	Agriculture	Industry	Services
Algeria	29.2	13.8	57.0	2.0	3.8	9.3
Egypt	29.2	13.3	57.5	3.9	5.1	15.4
Morocco	40.2	23.4	36.4	10.0	19.1	19.9
Tunisia	9.4	46.5	44.1	1.5	17.3	11.5
Islamic Republic of Iran	17.9	56.8	25.3	5.0	25.7	12.5
Iraq	19.9	28.4	51.7	1.7	5.1	6.5
Israel	8.0	17.1	74.9	24.3	13.9	39.9
Kuwait	0.1	5.5	94.4	-	1.2	10.2
Lebanon	23.6	20.0	56.4	20.5	13.5	17.8
Saudi Arabia	81.5	3.3	15.2	5.6	1.2	3.0
Syrian Arab Republic	67.7	13.1	19.2	13.9	6.7	7.1
Turkey	86.1	3.0	10.9	47.3	9.1	20.1
Jordan	25.0	26.1	48.9	4.2	4.3	8.5
Libyan Arab Jamahiriya	12.6	40.9	46.5	1.8	8.8	4.6
Yemen Arab Republic	83.3	5.1	11.6	4.4	2.7	4.0
Democratic Yemen	78.3	4.3	17.4	5.9	1.5	4.3

Source: ILO, 1977.

cheese, weave the tents, as well as clothes, furnishings and sometimes carpets, and are in charge of all domestic tasks.

Beck (1978, p.352), suggests that among Pashqa'i pastoralists in Iran,

> The role of the female in these household activities can by no means be considered here as subordinate, for she is an integral member of the household in its division of labour during the different stages of her life cycle. Learning tasks begins at a very young age (earlier than for the male). Her work is respected and regarded as vital to the economic unit; no household can exist without her labour.

The same author provides us with all the information we need to understand the nature of female subordination: women are exchanged at an early age between male-headed households, the more common form of marriage payment is bride price, residence is always virilocal, women have no inheritance rights and are primarily valued for their fertility particularly when giving birth to a male child, in a context where family and lineage strength are crucial. Age-sex hierarchies persist.

The status of these women is further constricted in the process of full integration into the market economy, not because they lose a more egalitarian status, but because the very basis of tribal reproduction breaks down (Kandiyoti, 1985), and the existing sexual divisions of labour are reinforced.

The spread of commercial agriculture has created further pressures through the expansion of cultivable land and soaring land prices. As market forces intrude on the local economy, self-sufficiency is lost and increasing socio-economic differentiation within the tribe makes its appearance or more specific the appearance of the peasant village. The organisation of the peasant village could range from landowned villages with peasant sharecroppers to relatively homogeneous peasant-proprietor communities. Here again, women's status must be understood primarily with reference to their place in the highly patriarchal kinship system- already spelt out in some detail- and their life-cycle in the patrilocal extended household, rather than the specific nature of their productive tasks (Kandiyoti, 1988).

The effects of rural transformation on women according to Kandiyoti (1985, pp.84-85), are neither unidirectional nor automatic but depend on different modalities of market integration, which may result in either the marginalisation of women's input into production in some cases, or its intensification in others.

An interesting example of such fluctuation is provided by carpet-weaving in the Islamic Republic of Iran (Beck & Keddie, 1978). Carpets were traditionally produced in the home for domestic use.

Western demand for Persian carpets encouraged the setting up of large workshops by Iranian and Western businessmen. For a while the number of large workshops grew, when recently the trend was reversed. The declining profitability of carpets compared with other forms of investment, and factory legislation enforcing compulsory employer welfare contribution and banning child labour, produced a return to the putting-out system, employing village women and girls whose labour is cheapest. This is a tendency which typically brings about an intensification of women's labour.

Male out migration presents another issue of labour intensification, which is frequently accompanied by a breakdown of rigid sexual division of labour in production as women come to take over male tasks.

Myntti's study (1979) of Yemen and more specific in Hujarriya, shows that male migration is high, labour shortages and mechanisation have had a major impact both on the division of labour in farming activities and on off-farm employment patterns. In sorghum cultivation women carry out the bulk of the agricultural tasks: planting, thinning, weeding, harvesting, winnowing, applying manure, etc.

The ploughing and threshing is still carried out by older men, although women may assume even these traditionally male tasks. When farm machinery is introduced, since the mechanised tasks are typically 'male', the women's work burden remain unrelieved. The shortage of male labour in Hujarriya has drown women into wage-work alongside men in the construction of irrigation networks; their wages are however, half those of men. Women also work both for wages and as family labourers in the cultivation of cash crops such as cotton and vegetables (Myntti, 1979, p.43).

In terms of marginalisation of female labour Friedl's analysis (1981) is the most representative. Caught in a cycle of indebtedness, a growing number of peasants could not get their subsistence from agriculture and had to enter wage labour and salaried employment in or outside the village. At this time, food imports and inflation led to a steep decline in agricultural production. With the decline, women who played an important role in traditional production were edged out and their work became confined to the most basic of housekeeping tasks. Apart from a short-lived attempt at sugar-beet production, work opportunities for women failed to materialise and they became totally dependent on men's incomes to provide even the basic necessities such as food. With wage incomes and modernisation the economic standing of the family tended to be increasingly expressed by the display of wealth in a lower-middle class, urban-inspired fashion; women were becoming consumers (Friedl, 1981, p.18).

The specific patterns of women's contribution to agricultural production are quite easily traceable to the particular mode of transformation of the rural community. In Turkey, it is possible to detect both different types of retreat from production and different types of intensification of women's input into agricultural production (Kandiyoti, 1989).

Among smallholders who cultivate cash crops such as cotton, family labour, particularly the labour of women, is critical. Although the soil preparation and sowing are mechanised, operations as hoeing and harvesting are not and depend on the labour of women. This tends to aggravate the cleavage in the sexual division of labour, since men take over the mechanised tasks and the bureaucratic/commercial dealings, whereas women are confined to unskilled, unremunerated, seasonal operations. In the case of marginal or suboptimal holdings the situation is further aggravated, since below subsistence income from land has to be supplemented from other sources. It is generally the men who migrate in search of seasonal, or more permanent employment, leading to a marked 'feminisation' of agriculture (Kandiyoti, 1977, p.61).

When this happens in regions where labour-intensive crops such as tea, tobacco or hazelnuts are cultivated, even men's failure to secure alternative sources of employment does not bring about a more equitable sharing of production tasks. Paradoxically, this dependence on women's work, far from giving them greater autonomy, can only be sustained by means of a harsher and more violent subjugation of women.

It is though the economic and political bases of village patriarchy having been altered (as already seen in the prescribed cases), the ideological stance (see chapter five) remains the least resort for the continuing subordination of women.

CHAPTER FIVE

IDEOLOGICAL STRUCTURES AND PERPETUATING MECHANISMS
LEGITIMISING WOMEN'S SUBORDINATION BECAUSE OF THE
PARADOX - CONCLUDING REMARKS

E. Introduction

Despite important regional variations, the case studies analysed so far point to
some significant uniformities and similarities in the conditions of rural women in the
Third World. At the most general level, we can see that the context of age and gender
relations in rural households has undergone profound modifications related to
processes of incorporation, through either colonialism proper or the work of world
forces. Despite historically and regionally distinct patterns, it is possible to see how in
each instance existing gender relations and asymmetries have been built upon,
extended and often exacerbated. However, the reproduction of gender subordination is
by no means mechanical and can be seen to involve important modifications and
reinterpretations of the economic, political and ideological bases of male dominance.

Beyond these broadly defined similarities there are some important variations
stemming directly from culturally specific modes of control of women and of their
sexuality (i.e., family, community, legal, cultural and religious institutions). These
cultural or ideological factors mediate women's economic realities (i.e., rural women's
involvement in unpaid or paid agricultural work, in non-agricultural activities or
migratory movements) and tern them into concrete life options, as will be seen in the
following section.

E.1 Cultural Contexts

Perhaps the main difference among the geographic regions of Latin America,
Africa, Asia and the Middle East, as regards female labour force participation is the

definition of *masculinity* and *femininity* resulting in either favourable or unfavourable attitudes towards women, wives, or mothers who engage in economic activity.

It is a general belief among sociologists and anthropologists that cultural norms regarding the subordinate role of women in the family are embedded in ancient law and custom (Manderson, 1983) and thus the understanding of the dependency of women must be viewed in a historical context. Religion has played a major role in the current balance between the sexes. Thus contrary to the view that seeks to blame Islam for lowering the status of its women, evidence from Latin America and other societies indicate that the problem lies, not in any religious doctrine *per se* but with the interpretations and practice of religious precepts.

Youssef (1974) analysis of role themes in Latin America attributes the current division of roles in Chile or in Latin America more general, to the basic fabric of the society, which incorporates a patriarchal pattern inherited from Spanish culture and Roman Catholicism. Even though the Church did not sanction more libertine and aggressive behaviour by men, the message to women was that their mission in life was above all to be 'good' mothers- 'good' in this case means the demonstration of self-denial, passivity and resignation or in other words being personified in the image of the Virgin Mary (Arizpe, 1982). Together, the influences of Catholicism and the Spanism and Moorish culture (Youssef, 1974) have resulted in a value orientation which includes the 'sense of subordination or hierarchy' (p.179). The hierarchical structure defines the superiority of men over women and encourages the perception that a woman's worth lies solely in her maternal role and her sacredness or purity.

To protect them from sexual aggression and safeguard their purity, women are confined to the home and restricted from any activity outside the home. This ideology of male dominance, known commonly in Latin America as the *machismo* cult, emphasises that woman's first responsibility as the caretaker of the home and discourages women from combining any type of economic activity with the care of her husband and children. Within this value orientation, status for the women is achieved only by producing children, preferably more males than females, while for men the presence of children (they fathered) in more than one household provides substantial proof of their protency and therefore enhances their status (Arizpe, 1982).

The ideology of male supremacy is not confined to the Latin American societies: it prevails in many other societies, albeit at varying degrees. As in Latin America, preference for male children characterises Sub-Saharan Africa; but the norms that define the role of women in the family differ between the two regions in a number of ways. The role of the Ghanaian women, for example, can hardly be described as limited to serving as wife and mother, since from pre-colonial times family life in Ghana has thrived on a sexual division of labour in which women performed essential economic functions. Even married women, (see chapter three) are observed to be economically active *in their own right and not merely as auxiliaries for their husbands* (Smock, 1977, p.177). Despite a cultural diversity emanating from the presence of numerous ethnic groups, all women expect to work and are motivated to do so because, typical of the predominant West African pattern, spouses maintain independent budgets (Smock, 1977) and wives are required to assume part of the burden of the support of the household.

Even in a society like Ghana where the scope of women's activity and their financial responsibilities to the household do not vary significantly from the male members preference for large families, and preference for male children is evident. In contrast to Latin America, however, the preference for large families in West Africa is mainly to ensure the survival and continuation of the clan or lineage regardless of whether the kinship system of descent or inheritance is patrilineal or matrilineal. Differentiating the two contexts even further is the relative lack of concern with female virtue: this explains the absence of extensive regulation to isolate women from men in West Africa (Smock, 1977, p.176).

In many respects, the cultural context in which women operate in West Africa is similar to that of south-east Asia women, and particularly Indonesian women. Kinship systems found in Indonesia include the patrilineal, bilateral and several other variations of these systems. Irrespective of the type of system, in none of the many ethnic groups of Indonesia are women confined to the household. Members of both sexes are expected to engage in economic activity; and in the nuclear family both the wife and the husband bear the economic responsibilities of their households, but woman's role as mother is central. The centrality of the female role, even as the male role is valued, is, according to Tanner (1974), what defines the system in Indonesia as matrifocal. The centrality of the woman's role in Indonesia should, Tanner argues, be distinguished from the Anglo-American *momism;* among middle class whites women's considerable power over their offspring's which they themselves have created within the household as a means of counterbalancing their economic emotional dependence on their husbands, exists in the context of their powerlessness in the wider society. On the other hand, the culturally defined role of mother is powerful economically significant, and culturally central not merely in the family but within the kinship group (Tanner, 1974, pp.132-33).

Indonesia being an Islamic country (90 percent of the population are Moslems) the cultural definition of women's role in the family and in the extended family of kin's, as described by Tanner, is contrary to the common belief that Islam accords a low status to women. Indeed the case of Indonesia supports Taskiran's view that in the Arabian Middle Eastern countries where women are confined to their homes, it is *not Islam but distorting customs* (Taskiran, 1974, pp.55-56, quoted by Ahmed, 1982, p.156) which are responsible for theses practices.

In India the Hindu faith is predicated on an elaborate caste structure which requires one to act according to one's status at birth in order to be rewarded in a subsequent life. Hinduism is pervaded by notions of purity and pollution. Not only are members of lower castes polluting to higher-caste groups, but also women of all castes are seen as inferior in the sense of being more *unclean* than men. The Hindu religion dictates that women should never be allowed to have independent lives and always to come under the jurisdiction of a man.

Women are supposed to be so devoted to their husbands that until its formal abolition in the colonial period, *suttee,* a custom whereby widows were required to throw themselves upon their husband's funeral pyre, was widely practised. Some widows climbed up willingly; other had to be tied down. The rationalisation was that a widow, by sinning in a previous life, caused her husband to die first. Her death also gave the husband's male relatives undisputed influence over the children and precluded her lifetime rights in the estate (Huber, 1991, p.36).

Although *suttee* and other discriminatory practices were abolished (i.e., female infanticide), Liddle and Joshi (1986, quoted in Brydon & Chant, 1989, p.40), pointed out that their abolition were not due to real concern about women's emancipation on the part of the British, but instead derived from first, a sense of moral outrage, and second, the need to find political ammunition for their refusal to grant India's right to self-rule. This is born out by the fact that in certain areas such as land reform and personal law, British activities had very deleterious effects on women such as the effective destruction of matriliny among the Noyars of Karala (Liddle & Joshi, in Brydon & Chant, 1989).

But *suttee* was not the only difficulty for Hindu women. In recent years for example, there has been a massive increase in bride deaths, both in South Asia itself and amongst Hindu communities abroad (Sharma, 1984). Bride death occurred when a girl's parents can not or will not meet the dowry payments required by the groom's family. Dowry is usually negotiated around the period of betrothal, but many authors have noted that there is an upward spiral of demands over time, reflecting the fact that wives are eminently dispensable and easily replaced (reinforcement of polygamy). Despite the fact that an Act of 1961 made dowry transactions a criminal offence, official action is rarely taken to protect women in these circumstances and police officers are wont to ignore even blatant incidence of violence (Kishwar & Vanita, 1984; quoted in Brydon & Chant, 1989, pp.1-45).

Additionally China sharing similar forms of production with India controlled women's behaviour with the ancient custom of footbinding. The rationale for the custom was that the resulting hobbled gait so tightened the muscles in the genital region that sleeping with a woman with bound feet was like sleeping with a virgin.

Western physicians report that no evidence supports such a belief. Whatever the rationale, women with bound feet certainly did little running around (Huber, 1991).

The mother applied the bindings when the little girl was three to five years old, depending on how small a foot was desired. The richer the family, the less work she would have to do, and the smaller the foot could be. Rich women were so crippled that they could not walk at all. The pain resulted primarily from bending the four smaller toes underneath the foot, then successively tightening the bindings until the broken toes atrophied.

The custom was widespread, especially in the colder and drier regions of the north where wheat was the main crop. In the south where rice, a much more labour-intensive crop was the main staple, the entire family was needed to in the paddies. Early in the industrial period, opposition to the custom increased (Huber, 1991, p.45).

In terms of Islam the practice of *seclusion* and the *veil* exist in Turkey only to limited degree, compared to other Muslim countries. The cultural context in which women operate in Turkey reflects differently some aspects of the Arabic culture and the practice of the Islamic religion. Despite the series of attempts by Turkey's governments to abolish some of the practices responsible for the low status of women, negative attitudes towards female employment outside the home persist in some segments of society. In comparison to neighbouring countries, the Turks are identified as the last of the Middle Eastern people to convert to Islam and yet as the people who developed the institute of *harem* to the most extreme point, to the extent that women were considered purely as sex-objects and as reproductive *machines* (Ahmed, 1982). In addition, women, especially those in the cities, were almost exclusively confined to their homes; male children are still preferred; and girls are taught the *womanly virtues of discretion; chastity and obedience* (Cosar, 1978, p.125).

The traditional expectations of the woman's role in the family varies by social class and area of residence. While fulfilment of the role of homemaker is expected of women of all classes, adherence to the cult of the veil and its other implications of exclusion is class specific. For the peasant women, farm work is compulsory: for this group of women the traditional responsibilities to the family and society at large are the combined roles of homemaker and farm worker. In contrast, women in the large cities continue to benefit from the various attempts by government to institute reforms. These women, therefore, have the unique opportunity to function in any capacity and to function in fields other than the strict traditional one. But the way of life of the women in small towns resembles closely the segregated *harem* life; partly due to a resurgence of religiosity (Cosar, 1978).

According to Fatima Mernissi (1985) women in the Arab World are not only segregated from men, but are also frequently subject to seclusion or *purdah*. Mernissi suggests that the fundamental rationale behind female subordination is that men are seen to need protection from women. Muslim women are regarded as extremely powerful, capable of making men use their reason through *fitna* (disorder or chaos provoked by sexual attraction) and threatening in terms of their potential to divert men's devotion from Allah.

Marriage is compulsory and polygamy permitted. Polygamy is an extremely significant variable in the equation of female subordination and male privilege: married women also see their co-wives as rivals thus preventing the development of any genuine female solidarity (Mernissi, 1985).

Aside from restricting women's mobility seclusion (purdah) involves the wearing of long concealing garments or a veil. The primary function of the veil is to ensure modesty and to limit women's contact with all men other than their own husbands or male kin (Minces, 1982). The veil also symbolises the invisibility of women in *male spaces* such as the street or public places (Mernissi, 1985).

The other practice, which has become equated in the West by Islam, but which is by no mean a Muslim institution, is female *circumcision* (Minces,1982, p.98). Termed by some *genital mutilation* circumcision is often argued to reduce women's sexual desires there by ensuring pre-marital chastity and conjugal fidelity. Even though education and social change appear to be sensitising people to the medical, if not psychological harm done by the custom the majority of families in Egypt still impose upon young female children the barbaric and cruel operation of circumcision (El Saadawi 1980, p.34; quoted in Brydon & Chant, 1989, p.30).

One of the few countries in the region which has attempted to *raise status* of women is Iran (Afshar, 1985, p.176). Due to dramatic and fluctuating changes in terms of legal and social position in Iran, in 1936 women were compulsory unveiled, making it one of the first countries officially to outlaw the veiling of women (Afshar, 1987). The Shah felt that the seclusion of women resulted in a waste of half the century's productive resources and called for the participation of women in the wider social and economic life; this began a long process of relaxation in some of the major constraints and restrictions placed on Iranian women (Afshar, 1987). For example, the Family Protection Law of 1967 prohibited men from taking multiple wives. The law also granted women the right to ask for a divorce in the event of their husbands bringing another woman into the home (Afshar, 1985). However, the social position of Iranian women consistently lagged behind changes in their legal status, and women could still, for example be prevented from working by their husbands if their employment threatened to disrupt the smooth running of the family home (Pakizgi, 1978). Furthermore, as the London Iranian Women's Liberation Group (1988, in Brydon & Chant, p.38), point out, women's emancipation under the Shah was foisted on them *top down* to suit the needs of the regime and not out of any genuine concern for women *per se*.

Gender inequalities have intensified since the revolution of 1978-9 where emphasis on Islamic fundamentalism has meant that women have returned to wearing the veil (*chador*) and given up a number of freedoms. In addition, some women under Khomeini have been executed for adultery and prostitution (Afshar, 1987).

As Halel Afshar (1987, p.83) points out:

> The Islamic Republic in Iran has created two classes of citizen; the male who benefits from the provisions of Islamic law and justice, and female who does not with the sole exception of the right to vote. Iranian women are in all other respects formally recognised as second-class citizens who have no place in the arena and no security in the domestic sphere. The husband has become the absolute ruler, entitled to exercise the power of life and death in his own home...

Iranian women have nothing to loose and everything to gain by opposing the
regime and its dicta concerning women.

To conclude, in all case-studies changes in the situation of women are still under way. In general though, some basic cultural elements which inevitably influence prevailing attitudes concerning the dimensions of women's role as economic units within the family in relation to their roles as mothers and wives persist. There are a variety of contexts in which women work. As long as there is the need to combine the two roles women will be faced with role incompatibility which means low rates of participation in the labour force and consequently low status within the domestic sphere. This is due to patriarchal and ideological constraints, as already described which influence and subordinate the levels and patterns of female economic activity.

REFERENCES

Abercrombie Nicholas, Stephen Hill, and Bryan S. Turner (1988): *The Penguin Dictionary of Sociology* (1984) 2nd ed. Penguin Books.

Afshar, Halah: *Women, Work, and Ideology in the Third World.* London: Tavistock. 1985.

Afshar, Haleh: 'Women, Marriage and the State in Iran'. In *Women, State and Ideology- Studies from Africa and Asia.* Afshar, H. ed. Basingstoke: Macmillan, 1987.

Agarwal, Bina: 'Women, Poverty and Agricultural Growth in India'. *The Journal of Peasant Studies,* Vol.13, No.4, July, 1986.

Ahmed, Leila: 'Feminism and Feminist Movements in the Middle East- A Preliminary Exploration: Turkey, Egypt, Algeria, People's Republic of Yemen. In *Women and Islam.* al- Hibri Azizah ed. Women's Studies International Forum. Oxford, New York: Pergamon Press, 1982, Vol.5, No.2, pp.153-68.

Alavi, Hamza: 'The Structure of Peripheral Capitalism'. In *Introduction to the Sociology of 'Developing' Societies.* Alavi, H. and Shanin, T (eds). London: Macmillan, 1982, pp.172-92.

Arizpe, Lourdes: 'Women and Development in Latin America and the Caribbean- Lessons from the Seventies and Hopes for the Future'. In *Development Dialogue,* Vol.1, No.2, 1982.

Barrett, Michele: *Women's Oppression Today.* London: Verso, 1980.

Barrett Hazel and Browne Angela: The Impact of Labour Saving Devices on the Lives of Rural African Women- Grain mills in the Gambia'. In *Different Places, Different Voices- Gender and Development in Africa, Asia and the Latin America.* Momsen H. J. and Kinnairo V (eds). London: Routledge, 1993.

Beck, Lois and Keddie, Nikkie: *Women in the Muslim World.* Cambridge, Massachusetts: Harvard University Press, 1978.

Beck, Lois: 'Women among Pashqa'i Nomadic Pastoralists in Iran'. In *Women in the Muslim World.* Cambridge, Massachusetts: Harvard University Press, 1978.

Bediako, Grace: *Male-Female Differential Status and Opportunity in the Labour Market- A study of correlates of occupational sex-segregation in Chile, Ghana, Indonesia and Turkey.* University of Pennsylvania, Unpublished Dissertation, 1988.

Beneria, Lourdes: *Reproduction, Production and the Sexual Division of Labour.* Mimeo, ILO, 1979.

Beneria, Lourdes: 'Sex Roles and the Division of Labour in Rural Economies'. In *Women in Rural Development- Critical Issues.* International Labour Force, Geneva: ILO, 1980.

Beneria, Lourdes and Gita, Sen: 'Accumulation, Reproduction, and Women's Role in Economic Development- Boserup Revisited'. *Signs, Development and the Sexual Division of Labour* (Special Issue). Vol.VII, No.2, 1981, pp.279-98.

Beneria, Lourdes: 'Accounting for Women's Work'. In *Women and Development- The Sexual Division of Labour in Rural Societies*. Beneria, L. ed. New York: Praeger Publishers, 1985.

Bennholdt-Thomsen, V: 'Subsistence Production and Extended Reproduction- A Contribution to the Discussion about Modes of Production'. *The Journal of Peasant Studies*, Vol.9, No.4, 1982, pp.241-54.

Bernstein, Henry: 'African Peasantries- A Theoretical Framework'. *The Journal of Peasant Studies*, Vol.6, No.4, 1979, pp.421-43.

Birdsall, N: 'Women and Population Studies'. *Signs*, Vol.1, No.3, 1976, pp.713-20.

Blumberg Rae Lesser: *Gender, Family, and Economy- The Triple Overlap*. London: Sage Publications, 1991.

Boserup, Ester: *Women's Role in Economic Development*. London: George Allen and Unwin Ltd. 1970.

Brydon, Lynne and Chant, Sylvia: *Women in the Third World- Gender Issues in Rural and Urban Areas*. London: Edward Elgar, 1989.

Caldwell, John C: 'A Theory of Fertility- From High Plateau to Destabilisation'. *Population and Development Review*, Vol.4, No.2, 1978.

Charles, Nickie: *Gender Divisions and Social Change*. London: Harvester Wheatsheaf, 1993.

Chayanov, A. V: *The Theory of Peasant Economy*. Illinois, R. D. Irwin Inc., 1966.

Coale, Ansley: 'The Demographic Transition'. *IUSSP* Paper presented at the Conference. Vol.1. Liege, 1973.

Collver, Andrew and Langlois, Eleanor: 'The Female Labour Force in Metropolitan Areas- An International Comparison'. *Economic Development and Cultural Change*, Vol.X, No.4, 1962.

Cosar, Fatma Mansur: 'Women in Turkish Society'. *In Women in the Muslim World*. Cambridge, Massachusetts: Harvard University Press, 1978.

Coulson, Margaret; Magas, Branka and Wainwright, Hillary: 'The Housewife and her Labour under Capitalism- A Critique'. *New Left Review*, Vol.89, January-February, 1975.

Croll, Elisabeth: 'Women in Rural Production and Reproduction in the Soviet Union, China, Cuba and Tanzania- Socialist Development Experiences. *Signs*, Vol.7, No.2, 1981a, pp.361-74.

De Beauvoir, Simone: *The Second Sex*. England: Penguin Books, 1974.

Deere, Carmen Diane and León de Leal, Magdalena: 'Peasant Production, Proletarianisation, and the Sexual Division of Labour in the Andes'. In *Women and Development- The Sexual Division of Labour in Rural Societies*. Beneria, L. ed. New York: Praeger, 1982.

Deere, Carmen Diane and León de Leal, Magdalena: 'Introduction'. In *Rural Women and State Policy- Feminist Perspectives on Latin America Agricultural*

Development. Deere, C.D and León, M (eds). Westview: Boulder, CO, 1987, pp.1-17.

Deere, Carmen Diane: 'The Division of Labour by Sex in Agriculture- A Peruvian Case Study'. In *Sociology of 'Developing Societies': Latin America.* In Archetti, E. P., Cammack, P. and Roberts, B (eds). Basingstoke: Macmillan, 1987.

Delphy, Christine: *Close to Home.* London: Hutchinson, 1984.

Durand, John: *The Labour Force in Economic Development- Comparison of International Census Data, 1946-1966.* Princeton: Princeton University Press, 1975.

Eisenstein, Hester: *Contemporary Feminist Thought.* London: Unwin, 1984.

Engels, Frederick: *The Origin of the Family- Private Property and the State.* New York: International Publishers, 1972.

Engels, Frederick: 'Women's Issue'. *Critique of Anthropology,* Vol.3, Nos.9 & 10 1979, pp.3-55.

Ettienne, Mona: 'Women and Men, Cloth and Colonisation: The Transformation of Production-Distribution Relations among the Baul'. In *Women and Colonisation: Anthropological Perspectives.* Ettienne, M. and Leacock, E (eds). Bergin Publishers Inc., 1980, pp.214-38.

Friedl, Erika: 'Women and the Division of Labour in an Iranian Village'. *MERIP Reports,* No.95, March-April, 1981.

Friedmann, Harriet: 'Household Production and the National Economy- Concepts of the Analysis of Agrarian Formations'. *The Journal of Peasant Studies*, Vol.7, No.2, 1980, pp.158-84.

Gita, Sen: 'Women Workers and the Green Revolution'. In *Women and Development-The Sexual Division of Labour in Rural Societies*. Beneria, L. ed. New York: Praeger Publishers, 1985.

Goode, William: *World Revolution and Family Patterns*. New York: The Free Press, 1963.

Gough, Kathleen: 'The Origin of the Family'. In *Toward an Anthropology of Women*. Reiter, R. R. ed. London: Monthly Review Press, 1975.

Handweker, W. P: 'Family Fertility and Economics'. *Current Anthropology*, Vol.18, No.2, 1977.

Harris, Olivia: 'Households as Natural Units'. In *Of Marriage and the Market*. Young, K., Wolkowittz, C. and McCullagh, R (eds). London: CSE, 1981.

Hartmann, Heidi: 'Capitalism, Patriarchy, and Job Segregation by Sex'. In *Capitalism Patriarchy and the Case for Socialist Feminist*. Eisenstein, R. Z. ed. New York: Monthly Review Press, 1979.

Hartmann, Heidi: 'The unhappy marriage of marxism and feminism- Towards a more progressive union'. In *The Unhappy Marriage of Marxism and Feminism*. Sargent, L. ed. London: Pluto, 1986.

Huber, Joan: 'The Theory of Family, Economy, and Gender'. In *Gender Family and Economy- The Triple Overlap*. Blumberg R. L. ed. London: Sage Publications, 1991.

International Labour Office: *Labour Force Estimates and Projections, 1950-2000*, Vols.I, II, III. Geneva: ILO, 1977.

Kandiyoti, Deniz: 'Sex Roles and Social Change- A Comparative Appraisal of Turkey's Women': *Signs*, Vol.1, 1977, pp.57-73.

Kandiyoti, Deniz: *Women in Rural Production Systems- Problems and Policies*. Paris: UNESCO, 1985.

Kandiyoti, Deniz: 'Continuity and Change in the Family'. In *Family in Turkish Society*. Turkish Social Science Association (eds). Ankara, Turkey: Erder, 1985.

Kandiyoti, Deniz: 'Bargaining with Patriarchy'. *Gender and Society*, Vol.2, No.3, 1988, pp.274-90.

Kandiyoti, Deniz: 'Women and Household Production- The Impact of Rural Transformation in Turkey'. In *The Rural Middle-East: Peasant Lives and Modes of Production*. Kathy and Pandeli Glavanis (eds). London: Birzeit University and Zed Books Ltd, 1989.

Long, Norman: *An Introduction to the Sociology of Rural Development*. London: Tavistock Publications, 1977.

Long, Norman: *Family and Work in Rural Societies. Perspectives on non- wage labour*. London: Tavistock Publications, 1984.

Mackintosh, Maureen: 'Domestic Labour and the Household'. In *Of Marriage and the Market*. Young, K., Wolkowitz, C. and McCullagh, R (eds). London: CSE, 1981, pp.48-67.

Manderson, Lenore: *Women's Work and Women's Role- Economics and Everyday Life in Indonesia, Malaysia and Singapore*. Development Studies Centre Monograph No.32, The Australian National University, Camberra: Helen Hughs, 1983.

Marx, Karl: *A Contribution to the Critique of Political Economy*. Chicago: Charles Kerr and Co, 1911.

Marx, Karl: *Capital* (Vol.I). Penguin Books, 1976a.

Melhuus, Marit: 'Cash Crop Production and Family Labour- Tobacco Growers in Corrientes, Argentina'. In *Family and Work in Rural Societies: Perspectives on non-wage labour*. Long, N. ed. London: Tavistock, 1984.

Mernissi, Fatima: *Beyond the Veil:* Male-Female Dynamics in Modern Muslim Society. London: Al Saqi Books, 1985.

Mies, Maria: 'Rural Women and the World Market'. In *Women and Development- The Sexual Division of Labour in Rural Societies*. Beneria, L. ed. New York: Praeger Publisher, 1985.

Mies, Maria: *Patriarchy and Accumulation on a World Scale- Women in the International Division of Labour*. London: Zed Books Ltd, 1986.

Minces, Julliette: *The House of Obedience- Women in the Arab Society*. London: Zed Books, 1982.

Molyneux, Maxine: 'Beyond the Housework Debate'. *New Left Review,* Vol.116, July-August, 1979.

Momsen, H. Janet and Townsend, Janet: *Geography of Gender in the Third World*. London: Hutchinson, 1987.

Moore, Bourington.: *Social Origins of Dictatorship and Democracy*. Allen Lane, Penguin Press: Harmondsworth, 1967.

Myntti, C: *Women and Development in the Yemen Arab Republic*. Eschborn: German Agency for Technical Co-operation, 1979.

Nash, June: 'A Decade of Research on Latin America'. In *Women and Change in Latin America*. Nash, J., Safa, H. et al (eds). Bergin and Garvey: London, 1986, pp.3-21.

Özbey, Ferhude: 'Socio-Economic Structures and Functions in the Family'. In *Family in Turkish Society*. Turkish Social Science Association (eds). Ankara, Turkey: Erder, 1985.

Pakizegi, Behnaz: 'Legal and Social Positions of Iranian Women'. In *Women in the Muslim World*. Beck, L. and Keddie, N (eds). Cambridge: Massachusetts, Harvard University Press, 1978.

Parsons, Talcott: 'The Social Structure of the Family'. In *The Family- Its Functions and Destiny*. New York: Macmillan, 1959.

Radcliffe, Sarah: 'The Role of Gender in Peasant Migration'. In *Different Places, Different Voices- Gender and Development in Africa, Asia and Latin America.* Momsen, H. J. & Kinnairo, V (eds). London: Routledge, 1993.

Sacks, Karen: 'Engels Revisited- Women and the Organisation of Production, and Private Property'. In *Toward an Anthropology of Women.* Reiter, R. R. ed. London: Monthly Review Press, 1975.

Sage, Colin: 'Reconstructing the Household: Women's Role Under Commodity Relations in Highland Bolivia'. In *Different Places, Different Voices- Gender and Development in Africa, Asia and Latin America.* Momsen, H. J. & Kinnairo, V (eds). London: Routledge, 1993.

Sahlins, M: *Stone Age Economics.* London: Tavistock, 1974.

Secombe, Wally: 'Housework Under Capitalism'. New Left Review. Vol.83, January - February, 1973.

_____: 'Domestic Labour-Reply to Critics'. *New Left Review,* Vol.94, November-December, 1975.

Sharma, Miriam: 'Caste, Class and Gender in North India'. *The Journal of Peasant Studies,* Vol.12, No.3, 1984, pp.57-88.

Smith, Joan and Wallerstein Immanuel: 'Households as an Institution of the World - Economy'. In *Creating and Transforming Households- The Contents of the World Economy.* Smith, J. and Wallerstein, I (eds). Cambridge University Press, 1992.

Smock, Audery Chapman: 'Ghana: from autonomy to subordination'. In *Women, Roles and Status in Eight Countries*. Giele Z. J. and Smock C. A (eds). New York: John Wiley and Sons, 1977a.

Stacey, Judith: *Patriarchy and Socialist Revolution in China*. University of California Press: Berkeley, CA, 1983.

Tanner, Nancy: 'Matrifocality in Indonesia and Africa and among Black Americans'. In *Women, Culture and Society*. Rosaldo, Z. M and Lamphere, L (eds). Stanford, California: Stanford University Press, 1974.

Tinker, Irene: 'The Adverse Impact of Development on Women'. In *Women and World Development*. Tinker, I. Bramsen, B. M. and Buvinic, M (eds). New York: Praeger Publishers, 1976.

Toffler, Alvin: *The Third Wave*. New York: William Morrow of Comp. Inc., 1980.

Townsend, Janet and Momsen, Janet: 'Towards a Geography of Gender in Developing Market Economies'. In *Geography of Gender in the Third World*. Townsend, J. and Momsen, J (eds). London: Hutchinson, 1987.

Turkish Social Science Association: *Family in Turkish Society*. Ankara, Turkey: Erder, 1985.

Walby, Sylvia: *Patriarchy and Work*. Oxford: Polity, 1986.